And God Created Wholeness

Catholicity in an Evolving Universe
Ilia Delio, General Editor

This series of original works by leading Catholic figures explores all facets of life through the lens of catholicity: a sense of dynamic wholeness and a conscious awareness of a continually unfolding creation.

Making All Things New: Catholicity, Cosmology, Consciousness
Ilia Delio

A New Heaven, A New Earth: The Bible and Catholicity
Dianne Bergant

The Source of All Love: Catholicity and the Trinity
Heidi Russell

The Image of the Unseen God: Catholicity, Science, and Our Evolving Understanding of God
Thomas E. Hosinski

CATHOLICITY IN AN EVOLVING UNIVERSE

And God Created Wholeness

A Spirituality of Catholicity

EDWIN E. OLSON

ORBIS BOOKS
Maryknoll, New York 10545

ORBIS BOOKS
Maryknoll, New York 10545

Fathers and Brothers
MARYKNOLL™

Founded in 1970, Orbis Books endeavors to publish works that enlighten the mind, nourish the spirit, and challenge the conscience. The publishing arm of the Maryknoll Fathers and Brothers, Orbis seeks to explore the global dimensions of the Christian faith and mission, to invite dialogue with diverse cultures and religious traditions, and to serve the cause of reconciliation and peace. The books published reflect the views of their authors and do not represent the official position of the Maryknoll Society. To learn more about Maryknoll and Orbis Books, please visit our website at www.maryknollsociety.org.

All scripture quotations are taken from the NRSV unless otherwise noted.

Manufactured in the United States of America.
Manuscript editing and typesetting by Joan Weber Laflamme.

Library of Congress Cataloging-in-Publication Data

Names: Olson, Edwin E., author.
Title: And God created wholeness : a spirituality of catholicity / Edwin E. Olson.
Description: Maryknoll : Orbis Books, 2018. | Series: Catholicity in an evolving universe | Includes bibliographical references and index.
Identifiers: LCCN 2017043170 (print) | LCCN 2018001596 (ebook) | ISBN 9781608337347 (e-book) | ISBN 9781626982680 (pbk.)
Subjects: LCSH: Religion and science. | Quantum theory. | Biology.
Classification: LCC BL240.3 (ebook) | LCC BL240.3 .O45 2018 (print) | DDC 261.5/5—dc23
LC record available at https://lccn.loc.gov/2017043170

Contents

Part II
Achieving Wholeness

Part III
Wholeness in Religion and Society

Acknowledgments

I am grateful for the inspiration and ideas from members of the Adult Spiritual Enrichment group at the Lamb of God Church as I developed the major book themes about science, religion, and spirituality, particularly Suzanne Bachman, Marilyn Bowman, Helen Byrnes, Judy and Marcel Charland, Judy Frye, Joanne Giguere, Connie Hutson, Dave and Linda Johnson, Jody Ladwig, Rev. Cliff Lawrence, Dr. Jim McMahon, Dr. Bill Nagy, Judith Olson, Rob and Sally Patterson, Rev. Anne Robbins, Ann Rupp, Tom and Carol Rutkowski, Stu Senneff, Joan Sturgis, and Sue Waldera. My good friends Tom Dunne, Andy Ezzell, and John Crowell have also helped me think about the integration of science and theology. Thanks to Kassie Cimmino and Tuesday Hadden for developing the figures in the book.

Over several years, the Adult Spiritual Enrichment group and I have been inspired by the writing and visits from Michael Morwood, John Crossan, and Bruce Sanguin and by the writing of Philip Clayton, Ilia Delio, Matthew Fox, Mary Harrell, Richard Rohr, and Francis Rothluebber, I am particularly grateful to Bruce Sanguin, who provided both a mystical and science-based path for my evolving spirituality.[1]

The work of Johnjoe McFadden and Jim Al-Khalili, quantum biologists and physicists, has provided a compelling model and

---

[1] Bruce Sanguin, *The Way of the Wind: The Path and Practice of Evolutionary Christian Mysticism* (Vancouver: Viriditas Press, 2015); idem, *The Advance of Love: Reading the Bible with an Evolutionary Heart* (Vancouver: Evans and Sanguin Publishing, 2012).

argument about how life is dependent on what happens at the quantum level.[2]

The models in this book are faithful to their quantum biological understanding of reality but also make room for nonphysical, nonmaterial consciousness and spirit, a model that represents the marriage of evidence-based rationality and the growth of trans-rational spirituality that is taking place in our culture.

I have been fortunate to have readers of the first draft who have made substantial contributions to my presentation. They are: Rev. David Cooper, Dr. Eric Dent, Dr. Charles (BillY) Gunnels, Dr. Mary Harrell, Rev. Cliff Lawrence, Dr. Eric Olson, Rev. Dr. James Reho, and Rev. Becky Robbins-Penniman.

I could not have written this book without the constant and loving support of Judith, to whom I dedicate this book.

---

[2] Johnjoe McFadden and Jim Al-Khalili, *Life on the Edge: The Coming of Age of Quantum Biology* (New York: Crown Publishing, 2014).

Worldview Assessment

Readers may wish to complete the following assessment before reading the book to gauge how closely their view of reality matches the worldview presented here.

Instructions: Select the one response to each statement you most agree with and circle the letter (A, B, or C). When you complete all four questions, count the number of A's, B's, and C's. Record the totals at the end of the statements.

Statements

1. My view of reality (what is real) is mostly based on

    A. what science has revealed
    B. what my religion has revealed
    C. an integrated view from both science and religion

2. I believe

    A. the only dimensions of reality are the physical dimensions revealed by science
    B. there is one supernatural dimension—God
    C. there are dimensions of reality beyond the physical dimensions

3. My focus is primarily on

    A. the material world I deal with every day
    B. the spiritual world
    C. linking the material and spiritual worlds

4. To develop as a person, I

    A. only need to deal with the circumstances of my daily life

    B. need to go inward to find wisdom and guidance

    C. need to integrate my daily activity and my spirituality

Totals: A's ____ B's ____ C's ____

Interpretation of Results

There is no best combination of numbers. Every person's worldview is respected and valued. Your worldview may be very appropriate and necessary for your personal situation.

If you have 3 or 4 A's, you may approach life with a strong orientation to a scientific worldview, meaning that you view reality as essentially knowable, even measurable. You believe any mysteries and unknowns are likely to become known over time.

If you have 3 or 4 B's you may approach life with a strong belief in God who, as well as being the creator of everything, has a continual presence in your life and the life of others.

If you have 3 or 4 C's, you may approach life with a belief that the reality you experience in your daily life has a deep and necessary connection to an inner source of wisdom.

Discussion of Results

The **C responses** represent the approach taken in this book. If that is your position, the book should increase your understanding of the necessary connection of the physical and the spiritual.

If you preferred the **A responses** or the **B responses,** this book may help you to engage in a dialogue with persons who have an opposing scientific or mystical/religious view of reality.

If you have a **2-1-1,** a **1-2-1 or** a **1-1-2** distribution of scores, it is likely that you are in the process of clarifying your view of the relation of science, spirituality, and religion, which means this book may be especially helpful.

Foreword

ILIA DELIO

I met Edwin Olson at the Chautauqua Institute a few years ago, shortly after he had contacted me about a book he was working on. A student of systems theory and process thought, Ed thought his book might fit into the Orbis series Catholicity in an Evolving Universe. I was reluctant at first to engage Ed's proposal, primarily because the series aims to bridge science and religion from a theological perspective. However, Ed was offering a different path into the discussion. His main interest, aligned with the series, is bridging the gap between science and religion by finding metaphorical bridges and mystical insights that move us beyond the impasse of dialogue toward a deeper integration of science and religion. He shows that the integration of science and religion is fundamental to our sense of reality because they are two faces of the same conjugate of knowing, as Teilhard de Chardin once remarked.

Our world today is fragmented and, in some respects, shattered, because we have split apart body, mind, and spirit. At the heart of this splintering is the entrenched gap between science and religion. We simply cannot transcend the impasse between these two fundamental areas. In the words of Albert Einstein, "Science without religion is lame, religion without science is blind." As such we are unable to live spiritual lives aligned with nature because we have no real sense of being part of nature; thus we have no real sense of a cosmic future.

This book is a holistic approach toward a renewed understanding of catholicity because it situates the human person in
the wider web of nature's relationships. Rather than beginning
with doctrines of faith or abstract theological concepts, the book
begins with biology and the new field of quantum biology. In a
sense, it begins with the book of nature. By explicating how our
bodies are dependent on quantum dynamics, we see how the
mystery of complexifying life emerges from and is dependent on
fluctuating fields of infinite possibilities. Olson offers us a wider
scope of understanding and a broader vision of our root reality.
We are wholes within wholes within wholes. He describes this
unfolding wholeness according to the layers of reality described
by quantum biologists: the surface reality of our traditional
world of objects and classical laws of physics and nature; a
middle stratum where there is turbulence and noise, mixed with
emotions, as we strive to know ultimate Reality; and a bedrock
stratum where life bubbles chaotically amid a sea of possibilities. Throughout these layers is the absolute divine whole, what
Teilhard called Omega, mysteriously hidden and entangled with
nature by way of consciousness, freedom, and love, empowering
nature's play among myriad possibilities.

Olson explores the primordial foundation of reality as consciousness and sees consciousness as the unifying bridge between
science and religion. Consciousness is the light that can enter into
the deeper, bedrock layer of reality and bring what is hidden to
the level of surface reality. Quantum consciousness is an important area of investigation today, and while it is still a new area of
study, the idea that consciousness works according to principles
of quantum mechanics indicates that consciousness is less about
structure and more about a flow of information. In this respect,
cross-fertilization among quantum physics, neurobiology, and Big
Bang cosmology is leading to a new understanding of consciousness as integral to matter, from the Big Bang onward. Consciousness may well be the bridge that joins science and religion, since
it undergirds evolution and may account for the fundamental
wholeness of reality. Olson brings together these ideas in a way
that spirit and matter take on new integrative meanings in light
of consciousness and in a way that is future oriented.

I encourage you to read this book thoughtfully, carefully, and
reflectively. If you are looking for a theological discussion on

wholeness, then this is not the book for you. However, if you want to widen and deepen your understanding of wholeness based on what we now know from biology and systems thinking, then you will appreciate Olson's efforts to illuminate catholicity as a principle of nature itself.

Introduction

> Religions claim to offer ways in which a Supreme Con-
> sciousness can be known in personal experience. The
> natural sciences are primarily concerned with . . . facts.
> For some, the findings of science point toward a Primordial
> Consciousness as the source and foundation of all things.
> For others, science promises to explain the cosmos com-
> pletely in material terms, without any reference to such a
> Primordial Consciousness. One of these views is correct.
> Which one? That remains the biggest question of all.[1]

Keith Ward, an Oxford professor of divinity, poses the question:
Is there a Primordial Consciousness in the universe? My response
to that question is not a yes or no choice. I argue that an underlying dynamic of wholeness is "the source and foundation of
all things" that Ward refers to. This wholeness encompasses our
physical, mental, and spiritual realities.

Understanding this dynamic wholeness in the universe deepens
both faith and science perspectives. Whether the deepening will
result in a reconciliation or only a greater mutual respect between religion and natural science remains to be seen. Whatever
the case, I hope that what is presented about wholeness in this
book will have a positive impact on individual lives, relationships, communities, and societies.

My challenge in writing about the "big question" has been to
maintain a ground that is credible to readers who have strong
beliefs in the primacy of the material basis of science and also

---

[1] Keith Ward, *The Big Questions in Science and Religion* (West
Conshohocken, PA: Templeton Press, 2008), 271.

1

credible to the religious readers for whom the essence of reality is spirit. In my experience, neither side easily changes its beliefs.

Some people are able to affirm both metaphysical positions of science and religion but maintain each as two separate magisterium, as two separate ways of thinking about and experiencing reality. This was made clear to me recently when I co-led a workshop with a scientist who was also a devout Christian. We got along fine if we talked about either science or religion. When I began to talk about the similarities between the natural sciences and spirituality, my science colleague became very uncomfortable. Any integration of the two domains was seen as not verifiable, and my colleague shut down.

My discussion of integrating science and faith is mystical and metaphorical, which should be useful for advocates of both domains to consider. I use the science of quantum biology to explain how life, including our bodies, is dependent on quantum dynamics. I use metaphor to speculate how our consciousness (mind) and our spiritual (soul) dimensions may be dependent on similar dynamics.

What Is the Current State of the Relation of Science and Religion?

In 2009, Alister McGrath, a professor of theology at King's College in London, was optimistic that there was a growing willingness on the part of "empirical, nondogmatic scientists" to consider the metaphysical and religious implications of the scientific enterprise that has created new and exciting conceptual possibilities. He believed this was also matched by an increasing awareness within the scientific community that the "scientific view of the world is hopelessly incomplete" and that there are "matters of value, meaning, and purpose that are outside science's scope."[2]

For a long time science has used models that purport to explain everything but have ignored levels of reality that mystics

---

[2] Alister E. McGrath, *A Fine-Tuned Universe: The Quest for God in Science and Theology* (Louisville, KY: Westminster John Knox Press, 2009), 221.

and persons of faith have experienced for millennia. Persons who understand the divine presence in mystical ways, using such terms as Love-Energy, are comfortable with how the Divine is immanent in physical reality.[3] They consequently have little trouble with appreciating the new discoveries of science. Many scientists, on the other hand, even though the origins of quantum mechanics and phenomena in the galaxies are inherently mysterious and unknown, cannot cross the boundary to call anything divine. Some scientists[4] go so far as to say that the awesome scientific phenomena are sacred.

Adam Frank, an astrophysicist at the University of Rochester, argues that "religious experience is an encounter with the sacred character of being" and that, by revealing the miracles that lie beneath everyday moments, "science is a gateway to an experience of the sacred." He believes that religious myths and scientific narratives both address "the world's unseen but deeply felt powers."[5] Issues about whether there is a transcendent reality "do not need to be resolved to begin developing a language that harmonizes science and spiritual endeavor."[6]

Contributing to the development of that discussion is a major goal of this book.

What Is a Way Forward?

Recently, Diana Butler Bass has argued that although there is evidence for religious decline across the West, around the planet there is a shifting conception of God. This is the path of mystics—the "personal, mystical, immediate, and intimate is

---

[3] Francis Rothluebber, *Who Creates the Future: Discovering the Essential Energy of Co-Creation* (Idyllwild, CA: WomanSpace, 2016).

[4] Adam Frank, "Can Science Be Sacred?" NPR's 13.7 Cosmos and Culture blog (January 20, 2012); Stuart Kauffman, *Reinventing the Sacred: A New View of Science, Reason, and Religion* (New York: Basic Books, 2009); Ursula Goodenough, *The Sacred Depths of Nature* (New York: Oxford University Press, 1998).

[5] Adam Frank, *The Constant Fire: Beyond the Science and Religion Debate* (Berkeley and Los Angeles: University of California Press, 2009), 259.

[6] Ibid., 260.

emerging as the dominant way of engaging the divine . . . to be able to touch, feel, and know God for one's self."[7] She says this is "a middle-ground revolution . . . a space between conventional theism and a secularized world . . . a path that enfolds the mundane and the sacred."[8]

John Philip Newell would agree that "at the heart of the physical is the spiritual . . . [that] hidden with the mundane is the Divine." He agrees with George MacLeod that what we do to matter, matters: "what we do to matter, therefore—whether that be the matter of another's body in relationship, or the matter of the earth's body and how we handle its sacred resources, or the matter of the body politic, and how we honor the holy sovereignty of one another's nationhood—all of this relates to the Light that we worship in the Christ child."[9]

In the workshops I have conducted in churches and the Chautauqua Institution on the sacred in science and religion and on the subject of this book, I have found that the workshop participants were comfortable with metaphors as a way of looking at the reality described by both science and religion. They found the ideas about their integration to be acceptable and even inspirational.[10]

Metaphors are part of the process of science. When we try to grasp the meaning of equations, we must form mental pictures such as spinning balls and waves in water.[11] Similarly, when we interpret our religious experiences, we must use symbols, metaphors, and ideas that are acceptable to our culture, which significantly colors our interpretations.

In this book I indicate which sections are grounded in scientific research and which sections are faith-based arguments. For

---

[7] Diana Butler Bass, *Grounded: Finding God in the World—A Spiritual Revolution* (New York: HarperCollins, 2015), 9.

[8] Ibid., 25.

[9] John Philip Newell, *The Rebirthing of God: Christianity's Struggle for New Beginnings* (Woodstock, VA: Skylight Paths, 2015), 36.

[10] Edwin E. Olson, "The Sacred in Science and Religion" (paper presented at the International Society for the Study of Religion, Nature, and Culture, Gainesville, University of Florida, January 14–17, 2016).

[11] Alan Lightman, *A Sense of the Mysterious: Science and the Human Spirit* (New York: Pantheon Books, 2005), 47.

the metaphorical sections, which integrate science and religion (the material that made my science colleague uncomfortable), I hope the reader's imagination will be stimulated and that the different metaphorical images will provide new practical insights.

I consider the book to be a new story about the integration of science and religion that will provide a different way of engaging with contemporary issues. Looking at the world through a lens that merges the physical, mental, and spiritual may bring about a more constructive dialogue between persons who believe there is only a material basis of reality and those who believe that a divine presence underlies everything and possibly an integration of their views.

Peter Harrison in his historical review of the science-religion conflict[12] provides an alternative narrative to the "long standing historical myths" of science and religion. He concludes that any conflict or integration between science and religion will largely depend on how each of the "territories" is defined.

I define and focus on the territories and integration of quantum biology, consciousness, and spirituality to explore how they describe the dynamic wholeness in the universe and how the phenomena in each domain may be related, at least metaphorically, as our lives unfold in this technological and spiritual age.

This book explores the dynamic of what happens at the smallest scale of life—the cells, molecules, atoms, and their constituent parts; the electrons, neutrons, quarks, and so on—as a metaphor for what may be happening in our conscious and unconscious minds and in our spiritual life. By looking at the quantum scale of reality and the speed at which things happen there, we can get a sense of the underlying wholeness that affects life, mind, and spirit.

Much of the previous writing about the quantum level of reality and its relation to spirituality has been done from the perspective of quantum physics. When comparisons and assertions are made about human behavior and human organization using quantum mechanics, the claims are generally seen as farfetched. But biological findings about the quantum reality in living cells

---

[12] Peter Harrison, *The Territories of Science and Religion* (Chicago: University of Chicago Press, 2015).

have opened new ways of thinking about what happens in plants, animals, and humans.

The Quantum Biology Connection

The discoveries by quantum biologists and physicists of how life is dependent on quantum reality are the basis for a practical model and strong metaphor for understanding how the physical reality of our bodies, minds, and souls are intertwined.[13]

Scientists have found that life, as we know it, is dependent on the capacity of electrons and protons in the atoms in living cells to

- do two or hundreds of things at once;
- instantly affect others at great distances;
- tunnel through apparently impenetrable barriers.

Particles in our body occupy multiple states at once and interact inexplicably over distance; this makes many essential life processes tick. Luca Turin, a biophysicist at the University of Ulm, says: "Life's 4 billion years of nanoscale R & D will have engineered many miracles."[14] Turin believes quantum biology is at an early stage of inexplicable observations about life and human cognition.

This behavior at the quantum level provides a strong metaphor for understanding that all our endeavors—our body, our mind, and our soul—depend on a connection to a deep and ultimately mysterious level of reality. For example, the term *particle* used to describe the makeup of atoms in our body is already an analogy for mathematical formulas in physics.[15] I am using the quantum biology terms as further analogies for mind and soul.

---

[13] See Johnjoe McFadden and Jim Al-Khalili, *Life on the Edge: The Coming of Age of Quantum Biology* (New York: Crown Publishing, 2014).

[14] Luca Turin, *The Quantum World* 3, no. 3 (London: Reed Business Information Ltd., 2014).

[15] Heidi Ann Russell, *Quantum Shift: Theological and Pastoral Implications of Contemporary Developments in Science* (Collegeville, MN: Liturgical Press, 2015} , 39.

We often partition reality into inorganic material, living entities, consciousness, and spirit to try to understand it and see how it affects us and how we can control our lives, but at the base of all these distinctions is a wave of energy, information, and mathematics. The whole has parts and distinctions that are so well integrated that the whole appears to have no parts.

For scientists, this reality of a whole without parts is a challenge to a worldview that reality consists of infinitely small, observable, measurable objects. For persons of faith, this view of reality challenges a worldview that says there is a separate transcendent spiritual reality.

We can reach a point of dissolving the boundaries between matter, mind, and spirit once we realize that everything is a metaphor. Even the exact science of quantum mechanics, as predictable as it is, is a metaphor for the reality it is trying to describe. Its paradoxes are metaphors for the unknown infinite possibilities of our existence.

The Depth Psychology Connection

Depth psychology—the psychology of the unconscious—is a modern way of seeking to connect to the deep powers that are beyond our conscious control. The "Force" in *Star Wars* movies is a popular expression of these powers. As researched by Carl Jung and others in the analytical psychology field, much of this is beyond the purview of science, such as a focus on the soul and spirit through the depths of inner experience and unconscious motivation.

Depth psychology explores the unconscious realm of dreams to find what Jung calls "our greatest treasure, establishing connection to the deepest foundation of our being."[16]

"Dreams are a key to understanding the experiential origins of religious symbols, behaviors, beliefs, and practices."[17] Dreams stimulate our capacity for hope and imagination, envisioning

---

[16] Keiron Le Grice, *Archetypal Reflection: Insights and Ideas from Jungian Psychology* (New York: Muswell Hill Press, 2016), 3.

[17] Kelly Bulkeley, *Big Dreams: The Science of Dreaming and the Origins of Religion* (New York: Oxford University Press, 2016), 3.

possibilities beyond the limits of our sense of reality, and move us toward wholeness.

In experiencing the unconscious world, we develop knowledge of the whole mind (psyche), both consciousness and unconsciousness. We actualize our deeper identity—the self, the center of our being. We then overcome the danger of the one-sidedness of rational consciousness and reconnect to our instinctual roots, a reconnection to nature.

What Is Unique about This Book?

This book integrates a scientific and mystical/metaphorical way of looking at how life develops and thrives. The wholeness of this perspective provides a creative path bursting through boundaries within ourselves, between ourselves and others, and between humans and nature. This holistic perspective lets us appreciate the awesome complexity that is within us and around us. It is like a Magic Eye picture—we see patterns, connections, and meaning that were there all along but we couldn't see them until we looked more deeply. We often see the parts but not the Whole, the individual but not the Source, the connection between everything.

This book presents a model that is faithful to scientific evidence that also makes room for nonphysical, nonmaterial consciousness and spirit. The wholeness model represents catholicity—the dynamic wholeness, a conscious awareness of the kinship between whole and part in all its manifestations and how all things relate together in a continually unfolding creation.[18]

The wholeness I describe includes both contemplation and active engagement that are woven together in our lives.

How the Book Is Organized

The book comprises three parts.

---

[18] Ilia Delio, *Making All Things New: Catholicity, Cosmology, Consciousness* (Maryknoll, NY: Orbis Books, 2015).

Part I, The Models of Wholeness (Chapters 1–4), explores wholeness and catholicity and develops the wholeness model and the cycle of becoming model that link our outer world, daily physical lives, our mind (consciousness), and our soul to our inner world, an interior that is the source of our continual renewal. The chapters are written to appeal to the religious and spiritual of all persuasions, to a-theists who most value logic, evidence, and scientific ways of understanding reality, and to those who seek to understand the psychology of both the religious and the scientific.

Part II, Achieving Wholeness (Chapters 5–8), applies the models to instances and examples of how our individual and collective realities can be changed and new realities created. Our daily physical, mental, and spiritual lives; our relationships; our institutions; and our communities—all can use the models to create new patterns of well-being and justice. The topics in Part II and Part III are inspired by Matthew Fox's call to awaken Deep Ecumenism, Deep Ecology, Deep Economics, and Deep Education.

> Not ecology as we know it; not education as we know it; not economics as we know it; not religion as we know it— none of these things is currently up to the task at hand. We need to go deeper . . . diving deep and surfacing. Moving inward and outward but always deeply. Deep where the joy resides; where the darkness, pain, and grief cry to us; where creativity is unearthed; where the passion for justice and injustice return again.[19]

Part III, Wholeness in the Future (Chapters 9–10), explores the implications for creating greater wholeness in religion and society. There is a global trajectory toward wholeness; perhaps the theory, models, and practices presented in the preceding chapters can contribute to that trajectory.

---

[19] Matthew Fox, *Meister Eckhart: A Mystic Warrior for Our Times* (Novato, CA; New World Library, 2014), 275–81.

Part I

Models of Wholeness

Chapter 1, "Three Dimensions of Wholeness," shows how life is connected to the deep levels of quantum reality. By analogy, this deep level of reality is like the deepest levels of consciousness and divine energy that are celebrated by all the religions of the world. Although there is only one Reality, it is necessary and useful to think of reality in separate dimensions that are intertwined. In the model I distinguish among the dimensions of body, mind, and soul.

The deep interconnection of these dimensions continually changes our lives. The information generated by their interactions "allows us to do new things that we had previously not even imagined."[1] The reality in these dimensions includes our values, our emotions, "our tears and laughter, gratitude, and . . . altruism, loyalty and betrayal, the past that haunts us and serenity. Our reality is made up of our societies, of the emotion inspired by music, of the rich intertwined networks of the common knowledge that we have constructed together."[2]

Chapter 2, "The Strata of Wholeness," explains the three strata and the core in the wholeness and the cycle of becoming models.

Surface. This is the stratum with which we are most familiar. It is the macro everyday world of physical objects, people, nature, and the universe where physical objects and behavior can be observed, measured, and predicted (at least with known probabilities).

---

[1] Carlo Rovelli, *Seven Brief Lessons on Physics* (New York: Penguin Riverhead Books, 2014), 27.

[2] Ibid., 75–76.

Middle. This is what is immediately beneath the surface. In our bodies this is the turbulent thermodynamic level of liquids and gases, the emotions, feelings, desires, and spiritual longings that propel action at the surface.

Bedrock. These are the atoms and molecules, dreams, and the deep beliefs we have in the goodness of the universe or God (if you are religious). At this stratum there is a quantum state where space and time are not relevant. The interactions here activate the strata above and add to the diversity of life. All journeys of development and creativity connect to this stratum to harness the energy of quantum possibilities and find the deep wisdom that is there. Every person, religious faith, and scientific theory has its own interpretation and explanation of what exactly happens at the bedrock level, but I argue that the phenomena are existentially, or at least metaphorically, the same.

Core. This level is not in the quantum biology model of Mc-Fadden and Al-Khalili, but I have included it because this is the realm of mystery, the source, the unknowable, the initial void, silence, and darkness before the development of quanta and the beginning of time and space as we know it. This could be the Big Bang, Apophatic Divinity, or an infinity of chaos, randomness, and uncertainty.[3] Whatever the case, this stratum of reality is the origin of the three strata of reality in the quantum biology model. Some believe it is possible to journey into this very deep reality as part of their meditative and spiritual practice. It is helpful to acknowledge and respect that there was (and is) a source, the ultimate Reality, of the three strata identified by the quantum biologists.

Chapter 3, "Spiraling through the Strata," sets the strata of the wholeness model into motion. Cycling through the strata increases our connectedness, wholeness, awareness, and capability of doing what is possible. We sometimes get stuck at one of the strata and try to abort the cycle of becoming, but the self-creating forces, the spirit, prompts us to keep cycling through all three strata and even the core. We arrive at new levels of seren-

---

[3] Edwin E. Olson and John D. Crowell, "Self-Creating and Quantum Theories of Human Spirituality: Developing a Unifying Narrative of Science and Religion," paper presented at the Conference of the European Society for the Study of Science and Theology, Lodz, Poland, 2016.

ity and resilience by spiraling through the strata of reality that compose our lives and drawing a conclusion. We move through the bedrock stratum of our physical body, our consciousness, and our spirituality, to the middle stratum of emotions and turbulence, and to the surface stratum of our everyday lives. In cycling through the strata we access the wisdom of others, find hard evidence, develop our own creative understanding, and rely on our own experience to arrive at a deeper understanding of the dimensions of any situation we face.

Multiple cycles become a spiral that we experience as progression. I illustrate the cycling process by using examples from the body, mind, and soul dimensions of the wholeness model.

Chapter 4, "The Wholeness Narrative," summarizes how the two models are learning models that can be used as methods for the development of any system—an individual, a group, an organization, or a society—to create a new reality rooted in wholeness.

Every day, new issues emerge that need our attention. The contemplation of wholeness at the bedrock and active engagement at the surface helps to identify what is significant and what needs our attention. The wholeness narrative has the capacity to handle the new conditions, greater flexibility, and additional layers of complexity of our modern age by accommodating and embracing other scientific, religious, and spiritual stories as explanations of wholeness that includes all fields of knowledge and all strata of being. Knowing what happens at each stratum of a system helps us to consciously work with the possibilities of transformation.

Chapter 1

Three Dimensions of Wholeness

Catholicity is the ever-evolving process of life that creates coherence. When we are coherent, we have health and integrity—we are whole. We attend to the "big picture," the picture beyond ego-gratification.

The "whole" of our lives is nested in the greater whole of the common good—the community, the nation, and the planet—a system of wholes. The greatest whole is the source of all wisdom. As we move toward greater wholeness at all levels, we move into more complete meaning, root causes, and greater complexity. We see the dimensions of reality and their relationship and realize there is always more beyond our understanding.

In this chapter I focus on the dimensions of body, mind, and soul that we often separate to emphasize their differences. In the following chapters I show how these dimensions intertwine to create a unity of spirit.

At the end of the chapter I present a model of the three dimensions—the wholeness model—that also includes the three strata of each dimension (surface, middle, and bedrock) and the core, which I describe in Chapter 2.

The wholeness model integrates the quantum biology theories about life with theories and practices of mindfulness and spirituality. As a result, the model transcends the differences among the three dimensions. Each dimension is in a creative relationship with the others. Because of these interconnections, quantum and nonmaterial processes in our body, in our consciousness, and in our spiritual life draw everything together into a coherent whole.

The Quantum Biology Model of Life
(The Body Dimension)

The quantum biology model of life at the edge of physical reality provides a strong metaphor for all aspects of our lives, including our physical being, our conscious awareness, and our sense of a transcendent spirit.

We are used to experiencing our living world within the four spatial measurements of length, width, height, and time as defined by the science of physics. However, as scientists have studied physical reality, concepts like matter, which were once defined within the physical domains of reality, are turning out to be manifestations of energy and information that establish a totally nonmaterial basis for existence.

Quantum physics explains that matter, often pictured as particles or tiny balls, is actually the manifestation of energy called quanta or packets of energy that emerge out of an underlying field like the electromagnetic field we experience every day. Physics is successful in explaining material reality because it focuses on *inanimate* things, which are relatively easy to measure. This has led to the assumption by some physicists that ultimate truth is to be found in inanimate things. However, biologists who study *living* things have found that living things such as a gene are much more complex than an atom and that living systems "might be employing some simple quantum information processing to improve their own efficiency."[1] Biologists have been able to demonstrate that the laws at work in complex living systems are not reducible to physics as we know it.[2] The emergence of novel changes in living entities cannot be predicted by any known physical laws.[3]

Jim Al-Khalili and Johnjoe McFadden, professors of theoretical physics and molecular genetics at the University of Surrey,

---

[1] Vlatko Vedral, "Quantum Information: Are We Nearly There Yet?" *New Scientist the Collection—Fifteen Ideas You Need to Understand* 2, no. 5 (2015): 128.

[2] Bernard Haisch, *The Purpose-Guided Universe: Believing in Einstein, Darwin, and God* (Franklin Lakes, NJ: New Page Books, 2010), 177.

[3] Stuart A. Kauffman, *Reinventing the Sacred: A New View of Science, Reason, and Religion* (New York: Basic Books, 2008), 37.

summarize recent discoveries of how life's most fundamental processes depend on a new understanding of the quantum world.[4] This new science of quantum biology is the study of how life sustains quantum mechanics at the edge between the quantum world and the deterministic physical theories of classical physics. In *Life on the Edge* they describe the three strata of life:

- *Bedrock*—the world of atoms and molecules and their particles in everything that obeys the precise and reliable rules of quantum mechanics.
- *Middle*—the thermodynamic layer of liquids and gases in living things, for example, our digestive juices.
- *Surface*—the macroscopic world of everyday objects such as trains, planets, and the cells of our bodies.

McFadden and Al-Khalili argue that life's roots reach down from the cells of living things on the surface through the turbulent middle thermodynamic layer to penetrate the quantum bedrock. This allows life to harness the strange quantum reality to allow enzymes to speed up chemical reactions in cells, photosynthesis to operate in plants, and mutations to occur in evolution (see Figure 1–1).

At its core, quantum biology recognizes the role that quantum particles could play in living systems. Instead of suffering from constraints imposed by the physical universe, the potential that living systems can take advantage of quantum process creates opportunities that were previously unappreciated. The quantum particles at the bedrock:

- can pass through apparently impenetrable barriers (*tunneling*);
- can be doing two or a hundred things at once (*superposition*);
- are connected and instantaneously affect each other at great distances (*entanglement*);
- cooperate in doing all of these things at once (*coherence*);
- decouple from such cooperation (*decoherence*).

---

[4] Johnjoe McFadden and Jim Al-Khalili, *Life on the Edge: The Coming of Age of Quantum Biology* (New York: Crown Publishing, 2014).

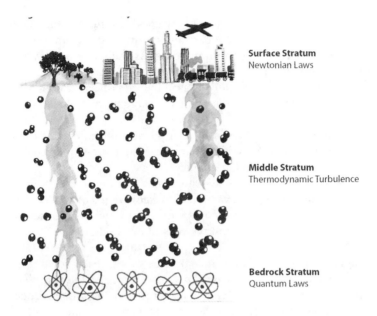

Surface Stratum
Newtonian Laws

Middle Stratum
Thermodynamic Turbulence

Bedrock Stratum
Quantum Laws

Figure 1–1. Strata of Reality

Tunneling—To pass through barriers, a particle must remain in a wavy state in order to seep through. Big objects are made up of trillions of atoms that cannot behave in a like fashion. Protons in an atom are like wavy clouds surrounding the tiny nucleus. These electron waves pass through energy barriers as sound waves pass through walls.[5]

Superposition—Electrons can vanish from one point in space and instantly materialize in another. Something happening "over here" has an instantaneous effect "over there," no matter how far away "there" is. Electrons and protons can vanish from one position in a brain and instantaneously rematerialize in another part of a brain. For example, European robins can sense the

_____

[5] This may explain how billions of protons in the cells within a tadpole work together to tunnel through strong, long ropes of proteins and accelerate the production of a frog. The vibrations of the tadpole's enzymes bring atoms and molecules into close enough proximity to allow electrons and protons to quantum tunnel (McFadden and Al-Khalili, *Life on the Edge*, 67).

earth's weak magnetic field and draw directions from it by an inbuilt chemical "compass." As they migrate, they can distinguish between pole and equator as their compass "measures the angle of dip between the magnetic field lines and the surface of the earth."[6]

Entanglement—Experiments have shown that pairs of photons separated by hundreds of miles influence each other. When one photon's polarization is pointed up, the other's polarization was found to point down. As with superposition, something happening "over here" has an instantaneous effect "over there," no matter how far away "there" is. If all hundred billion neurons in a human brain are entangled, they may be binding together all of the information encoded in separated nerves and provide the conscious mind with the powerful capabilities of a quantum computer.

Coherence—At the molecular level biological processes are very fast (trillionths of a second) and are confined to short atomic distances. This requires unified action (cooperation) among the atoms. This is *coherence*—a circumstance where large numbers of particles cooperate. When tree leaves capture photons from the sun, they are dependent on a delicate coherence that can be maintained for biologically relevant lengths of time within the highly organized interior of a leaf. Life bridges the two realities—the physical leaf we see and the unseen quantum bedrock. As an analogy, we can think of the neurons in our brain linking together to form a coherent thought.

Decoherence—All atoms interact with trillions of other atoms all the time. This complex interaction causes the delicate coherence to leak away very quickly and be lost in the incoherent noise of its surroundings in the middle stratum. This is *decoherence*. A cell dies when its connection with the orderly quantum realm is severed, leaving it powerless to resist the forces of the thermodynamic middle stratum.

Al-Khalili and McFadden admit that there is a big puzzle at the heart of quantum biology. Physicists must cool down their experiments with inanimate objects to near absolute zero temperature and perform them in a vacuum to minimize the stormy molecular noise that would otherwise destroy delicate quantum

---

[6] Ibid., 6.

effects. How quantum phenomena that biologists have found are maintained inside warm, wet, and molecularly noisy living cells remains a mystery. However, the summary of research by Al-Khalili and McFadden presents plausible theories of how life navigates a narrow strait between the classical and quantum worlds. They call this the "quantum edge." Rather than avoiding molecular storms in the middle stratum, life embraces them, like the captain of a ship who harnesses turbulent gusts and squalls to maintain the ship upright and on course. As a result, quantum activity is able to affect life on the surface.[7]

Three billion years of natural selection have fine-tuned the evolutionary engineering to drive quantum systems to "dance" with the "noise" in the thermodynamics layer in a rhythm that is "just right" for maintaining life. Our living cells harness the thermodynamic storms—the molecular "noise" in the middle strata—to maintain their connection to the quantum bedrock. A team of physicists and complexity scientists support this theory with their discovery that some biological systems can stay in a quantum coherent state for a long time at room temperature if there is the right level of complexity between chaos and regularity.[8]

This hierarchical view of the physical and biological world, where every level depends on every other, provides a strong metaphor for the possibility that a vital human consciousness and a mature human spirituality also depend on a deep and strong connection to something akin to the quantum bedrock upon which life is dependent.

A living entity like a tree is dependent on the interaction of the molecules at a deep quantum level at the bedrock. A steam engine is only dependent on the thermodynamic activity in the middle (Figure 1-1).

In its evolution, nature has learned to create quantum states where advantage can be taken of the efficient, instantaneous, everywhere movement of the particles.

---

[7] Ibid., 305–10.

[8] G. Vattay, S. Kauffman, and S. Niiranen, "Quantum Biology on the Edge of Quantum Chaos," *PLoS ONE* 9, no. 3 (March 6, 2014): e89017. https://doi:10.1371/journal.pone.0089017.

Life senses the environment around it, and reacts and adjusts to the things its senses pick up. Life finds ways to reproduce itself. And somewhere along the way to creating these subtle and creative processes, evolution tried exploiting the quantum tricks available to molecules—being here and there at the same time or existing in entangled states where distant molecules affect each other's states. A few of these tricks worked, and were retained.[9]

As available quantum tricks were exploited by life, life's ability to maintain dependability and the variance needed to maintain coherence improved. This ability affects what does or does not happen at the surface. When in a coherent state, electrons and protons can "tunnel," taking all possible paths, without losing energy. At the quantum level space and time are not relevant, a facet of existence unimaginable to big objects like humans, but utterly normal for a subatomic particle.

For example, to achieve the efficiency of photosynthesis and metabolism, algae and plants (their evolutionary descendants) use quantum superposition to allow energy to "simultaneously travel along all possible paths to the reaction centre."[10] This allows the plants to take the energy of the sun and store it within their cells efficiently. "That stored energy is the basis of life on earth: almost every living creature is dependent upon the plants' harvest—a harvest that itself depends on quantum weirdness."[11]

As far as we know, there is only a single set of laws that govern the way the world behaves: quantum laws. "Newtonian laws are, ultimately, quantum laws that have been filtered through a decoherence lens that screens out the weird stuff."[12] Elementary particles are not building blocks of reality but are patterns of reality, patterns of a whole that does not have parts. Quantum mechanics is at the heart of the bedrock.

As the science of quantum biology progresses there are attempts to broaden the perspective of what coherence in

---

[9] Michael Brooks, *At the Edge of Uncertainty* (New York: Overlook Press, 2014), 147.

[10] Ibid., 156.

[11] Ibid., 157.

[12] McFadden and Al-Khalili, *Life on the Edge*, 132.

biological systems may mean and improve modeling of living systems. "There is accumulating evidence that at some level, biological organization" and dynamics "may display properties" like quantum coherence "that is not readily explained by classical means."[13]

The Mind Dimension

The quantum biology model explains how life in our bodies is dependent on quantum activity, but what about mind—our consciousness? How does the quantum biology model of life apply to understanding consciousness? Mind is certainly connected to the brain. Mind represents the more intangible functional aspects of the brain, "the subjective aspects of neural activity as opposed to the brain's 'objective' structure, physiological aspects."[14] The brain takes facts and integrates these facts with emotion.

With 10 billion neurons, our brains perform 10^{18} operations per second. Each cell in our body and each neuron in our brains is intelligent. Since they work together in as many as 10^{15} simultaneous processes at the bedrock, is it possible that quantum processes affect consciousness?

The brain itself doesn't produce consciousness. Ilia Delio describes consciousness as "the pattern of active relationship, the 'wave side' of the wave-particle duality" that emerges from the wholeness of the deeply entangled fields of energy.[15] These relationships include communication and the flow of information that is "made possible by overlapping waves or perhaps . . . overlapping energy states."[16] This traces the origin of our mental life back to the cosmic beginning and defines *mind* as an emergent

---

[13] Martin Robert, "A Broader Perspective about Organization and Coherence in Biological Systems" (Cornell University Library, 2013), http://arxiv.org/abs/1212.0334.

[14] Eugene C. D'Aquili and Andrew B. Newberg, *The Mystical Mind: Probing the Biology of Religious Experience* (Minneapolis, MN: Fortress Press, 1999), 50.

[15] Ilia Delio, *Making All Things New: Catholicity, Cosmology, Consciousness* (Maryknoll, NY: Orbis Books, 2015), 61–62.

[16] Ibid., 61.

process of communication and consciousness, where synthesizing activity occurs and self-awareness increases.[17]

In describing the mind, McFadden and Al-Khalili point out the consciousness of the Paleolithic artists who thirty thousand years ago smeared charcoal over the walls of the Chauvet-Pont-d'Arc Cave in France (discovered in 1994 by Jean-Marie Chauvet). But what is consciousness? Nobody knows where or how it fits in with a quantum perspective on life. Particularly, "how does complex neuronal information get glued together in our conscious minds to form an idea?"[18] This "is often termed the binding problem: how does information encoded in disparate regions of our brain come together in our conscious mind" to create a vision or idea?[19]

An analogy of how we interact with a computer may be helpful. Bits and pieces of information are stored in different areas of the memory that are observed as a single interface when we interact with it. Consciousness functions in a similar fashion by pulling all of the pieces of information into a single unified perspective that then also includes the extra dimension of independent thought and processing.

For the cave artists, McFadden and Al-Khalili ask, how does all the disparate blip-encoded information in their brains generate the unified perception of a bison and allow an artist to draw a charcoal image on a cave wall? They conclude: "This puzzle, variously referred to as the mind-body problem or the hard problem of consciousness, is surely one of the deepest mystery of our entire existence."[20]

Is consciousness a quantum mechanical phenomenon? McFadden and Al-Khalili write:

> If . . . connections between all the hundred billion neurons in a human brain were possible, then they could, potentially, bind together all the information encoded in separated nerves and thereby solve the binding problem.[21]

---

[17] Ibid., 66.
[18] McFadden and Al-Khalili, *Life on the Edge*, 238.
[19] Ibid.
[20] Ibid., 241.
[21] Ibid., 257.

Is it possible to have quantum coherence in the brain long enough to have any impact on brain computation? The authors discuss the possibility of electromagnetic fields and quantum coherent ion channels as a plausible link between the quantum and classical realms in the brain to explain consciousness, but they admit that there is no evidence that quantum mechanics is actually needed to account for consciousness, unlike other biological phenomena such as enzyme action or photosynthesis. But they add: "Is it likely that the strange features of quantum mechanics we have discovered to be involved in so many crucial phenomena of life are excluded from its most mysterious product, consciousness? We will leave the reader to decide."[22]

Michael Brooks says that

life has had billions of years to "discover" quantum mechanics. . . . Even if electrical impulses among neurons within the brain—something well described by classical physics—are the immediate basis of thought and memory, a hidden quantum layer might determine, in part, how those neurons correlate and fire.[23]

McFadden and Al-Khalili end their discussion of mind by returning to that dark cave in the south of France to complete the chain of events as the artist is "poised before the wall watching the torchlight flicker over its gray contours":

Some play of the light and rock brings the image of a bison to her conscious mind. This is sufficient to create an idea in her head, perhaps instantiated as a fluctuation of her brain's [electromagnetic] field, that flips open clusters of coherent ion channels in lots of separated neurons, causing them to fire synchronously. The synchronous nerve signals fire action potentials throughout her brain and, via synaptic connections, initiate a train of signals that travels down her spine and, via nerve-nerve junctions, to the motor nerves

---

[22] Ibid., 263.

[23] Michael Brooks, "Quantum Life," in *The Quantum World: Your Ultimate Guide to Reality's True Strangeness,* New Scientist: The Collection Book 3 (Reed Business Information Ltd.).

Figure 1–2. 30,000-year-old wall drawing in Chauvet-Pont-d'Arc Cave in France. Source: Museo de Altamira y D. Rodríguez.

that discharge their packets of neurotransmitters into the neuromuscular junctions that are attached to the muscles of her arm. Those muscles contract to generate the coordinated motion of her hand that sweeps across the cave wall, depositing a line of charcoal on the rock in the shape of a bison [see Figure 1–2]. And, perhaps more important, she perceives that she initiated the action *because* of an idea in her conscious mind. She is not a zombie. Thirty thousand years later, Jean-Marie Chauvet shines a torch on that same cave wall and the idea that came to life within the brain of that long-dead artist is once again flickering through the neurons of a conscious human mind.[24]

Recent research has revealed that animals, insects, plants, and even bacteria have a degree of consciousness. Here is a sampling of these findings from the most simplistic (automated action) to higher-level forms of processing that may approach consciousness:

---

[24] McFadden and Al-Khalili, *Life on the Edge*, 264.

- Bacteria will swim in a straight line as long as the chemical it senses seems better now than what it sensed a moment ago. If not, it prefers to change course.
- A Venus flytrap does not produce digestive enzymes until it counts more than three flicks of a trigger hair.
- The Mimosa pudica plant curls up its leaves in response to being touched, but "chooses" not to flinch when it "remembers" that the threat does no harm.
- As a young male zebra finch listens to his father's courtship song, networks of brain cells are activated that the younger bird will use later to sing the song himself.
- Prairie voles console one another when distressed.
- In captivity, octopuses have been known to identify individual human keepers and turn off lightbulbs by spouting jets of water.

How Does Consciousness Work?

Consciousness is a process of perpetual development. We are aware of the shifting patterns of our life when we are awake. We experience a succession of continuous moments that exist and then dissolve. We intentionally or unintentionally link these moments together in patterns to create our conscious reality. We assign both causation and meaning to these patterns. While awake, images and ideas come and go and combine and recombine, sometimes unpredictably.

When asleep, our unconscious mind descends into the unknown, the irrational, and to the illuminated source at the bedrock. The causation and meaning assigned in the conscious state dissolves.

An example of attaining coherence in a waking state: "What is the name of your third-grade teacher?" If we have an answer to that question (or remember the names of any of our teachers), it suggests that we store memories in a coherent state.[25] With the

---

[25] Dr. Eric Olson uses this example in teaching future science teachers at State University of New York (Oswego).

loss of that ability, as with Alzheimer's patients, we move into a decoherent state.

In an unconscious state, moments and events are in uninterrupted coherence, as are quantum particles in a coherent state when they tunnel, superposition, and entangle without any thought required. When awake and making meaning of the myriad images from the dreams and our thoughts before us, we both limit and interfere with this coherence. We lose the amazing, unmediated images and stories that appear in our dreams.

Our conscious self is "the source of free will and our capacity for rational analysis as well as soaring complex thoughts. It is not infinitely powerful. . . . Consciousness has definite limitations." Consciousness "rests upon a massive unconscious edifice millions of years in the making." An essential function of our consciousness is to limit what we take in from the universe, else we would be overwhelmed. But because it filters the information presented by the brain, "consciousness *feels* as if it contains everything we are and everything we can be. This is an illusion."[26]

Our unconscious mind contains an "amazing array of instincts and adaptations capable of immense creativity. It contains all the basic plans required for life on earth as *Homo sapiens* evolved in small foraging bands in the ancestral environment. . . . Instincts self-organize and manifest themselves" in ways beyond our conscious awareness.[27]

Our conscious mind "rests upon a field of consciousness that transcends the divide between the individual and the world. . . . The mind is where a sense of the whole—catholicity—becomes reality. . . . When the whole brain is enabling the whole person to connect to the whole environment, catholicity is alive."[28]

Entangled quantum variables may conceivably share some form of consciousness and free will, even thoughts and feelings, whether embodied in us, or in our collective unconscious, a space shared by all humans where symbols and ideas emerge.

---

[26] Eric D. Goodwyn, *The Neurobiology of the Gods: How Brain Physiology Shapes the Recurrent Imagery of Myth and Dreams* (New York: Routledge, 2012), 190.

[27] Ibid.

[28] Delio, *Making All Things New*, 150.

The Soul Dimension

The dimension of soul in the wholeness model is an essential addition to the quantum biology model of life. As humans gained self-consciousness, they recognized a spiritual dimension within their "self" as soul and the spirit outside of their "self" as a greater soul. As we became aware of what is distinctive about being human, we became aware that we are part of a divine world.

"The word *soul* is most often used to designate the spiritual reality of what is growing within us as we evolve."[29] Soul "is a positive, purposeful field of activity at the core of your being . . . that part of you that understands the impersonal nature of the energy dynamics in which you are involved, that loves without restriction and accepts without judgment."[30]

Marcel Gleiser offers a modern neuroscience-based concept of the soul: "What if we consider your soul as the sum total of your neurocognitive essence, your very specific brain signature, the unique neuronal connections, synapses, and flow of neurotransmitters that make you you?"[31] This suggests that spirituality can be described in scientific terms.

Many religions use the tree of life as a metaphor for a spiritual life that has roots reaching into a reservoir of living water. Just as the quantum bedrock is the source of matter, energy, and life, where quantum particles pop in and out of being in a field of creativity, the quantum bedrock is the Ground of Being, a term Paul Tillich used to describe God.[32] Soul, as our growing spirituality, fits in the quantum field theory of infinite possibilities in an entangled universe. For example, sometimes when we pray or meditate we get lost in awe and hope and enter the bedrock

---

[29] Steve McIntosh, *The Presence of the Infinite: The Spiritual Experience of Beauty, Truth, and Goodness* (Wheaton, IL: Quest Books, 2015), 176.

[30] Gary Zukov, *The Seat of the Soul* (New York: Simon and Schuster, 1989), 31.

[31] Marcel Gleiser, "Is Neuroscience Rediscovering the Soul," NPR 13.7 blog (April 5, 2017).

[32] Paul Tillich, *Systematic Theology*, vol. 1 (Chicago: University of Chicago Press, 1951).

of possibilities in a reverie until the field of possibilities collapses back into a reality we can take to the surface.

Reference to the Divine traditionally is hidden in murky, cloudy, and fleeting glimpses. In the Hebrew scriptures, God says the divine Name is "I am who I am"—an enigmatic moniker if there ever was one. In Proverbs and the Gospel of John, Wisdom (Sophia) and the Word were there from the beginning of creation. The breath of God is located everywhere. Jesus was constantly saying "the kingdom of God is like . . . ," and then giving many metaphors including yeast and a mustard seed.

None of these statements about the Divine provide a lot of clarity.

John Haught describes the language of theology and faith as inherently mysterious. Symbols, metaphors, and analogies that are used are vague and can be paradoxical.[33]

Heidi Ann Russell quotes Rahner, who defines spirit as the "dynamism that drives our lives and is our openness" to the "incomprehensible and mystery we call God." Spirit is the "infinite potentiality of the dynamism" of catholicity. Our soul is an embodied spirit.[34]

Catherine Keller describes the interconnection between apophatic theology and quantum physics where we find the same themes of contradictions and "epistemic uncertainty, ontological indeterminacy, rational contradiction,"[35] and where events that "take place very far apart seem to be entangled" because "both events form a single creative act, a single 'actual entity' arising out of a common field of potentialities."[36]

Using quantum biology as a metaphor for soul helps us to think and talk about the divide in theology between transcendence and immanence. If reality has no parts, can we make a

---

[33] John Haught, *Science and Faith: A New Introduction* (New York: Paulist Press, 2013).

[34] Heidi Ann Russell, *Quantum Shift: Theological and Pastoral Implications of Contemporary Developments in Science* (Collegeville, MN: Liturgical Press, 2015), 36.

[35] Catherine Keller, *Cloud of the Impossible: Negative Theology and Planetary Entanglement* (New York: Columbia University Press, 2015), 132.

[36] Ibid., 150.

distinction between what is divine and what is human? We can make a distinction if we want to talk about different aspects of our experience. But in so doing, we need to realize we are making distinctions to meet our need for understanding.

Finley Lawson points out that for persons of faith who recognize the reality of the quantum world, there is not a metaphysical gulf between divine and human.[37] There is no difficulty in combining spiritual and human material because they are ontologically the same; the division is one of epistemology. To understand how we can talk about God as part of a quantum understanding of the world, we need a theology that differentiates the patterns that describe the presence of the Divine and the patterns that are created by us, including how we influence others through our own spirituality.[38]

The soul dimension of the wholeness model embodies an evolutionary drive that transcends the polarities that Lawson describes.

Imaginal Reality

Borrowing the concepts of Henry Corbin,[39] Mary Harrell describes the realm of soul as the in-between dimension of matter (body) and mind. It is the psychological world of imaginal experiences and figures as ontological realities. Although common in religious discourse, the physical science community has not regarded such visions and dreams as real, only figments of a person's imagination. Harrell argues that with the emerging subatomic and cosmic models of reality (as I describe in this book) it is time to consider the imaginal as real.[40]

---

[37] Finley Lawson, "Complete in Manhood: Understanding Christ's Humanity in Light of Quantum Holism," paper presented at the ESSAT Conference in Lodz, Poland, April 2016.

[38] Ibid.

[39] Henry Corbin, *Alone with the Alone: Creative Imagination in the Sufism of Ibn'Arabi* (Princeton, NJ: Princeton University Press, 1997).

[40] Mary Harrell, *Imaginal Figures In Everyday Life: Stories From the World between Matter and Mind* (Asheville, NC: InnerQuest Books, 2015), 2.

Imaginal figures in our soul can be "inner" figures, unique to a particular person, or representations of "outer" figures that are experienced by many. Harrell describes the imaginal realm as a dynamic and real place of experience, a locus inhabited by multivocal, multivalent beings. She refers to them as interior figures and images that are neither fully matter nor fully spirit.[41] Carl Jung also spoke of imaginal figures as both personifications of internal (and often unconscious) dynamics and also as autonomous realities.[42]

Harrell says that imaginal figures can be investigated through dream figures, reverie, and active imagination—an act of directed wondering and listening while one is awake, deliberately breaking our habitual patterns of assigning cause and meaning to images and events.[43] During sleep our brain engages in a "variety of complex, dynamically interactive cycles of activity that involve many of the same neural systems considered essential to waking consciousness."[44]

This perspective helps us to consider that the beings we experience in our spiritual world are real, although we cannot say exactly what that world is like. We know it exists; how it exists is still a mystery.

Depth Psychology

Since the wholeness model rests on the deep numinous strata of reality I call the core, it is necessary to identify how one journeys to find truth in the hidden, dark, mysterious depth of the psyche, the inner person, explored by Jung, Harrell, and others. Jung named the deep place as the personal and collective unconscious. Compared to the conscious world at the surface, which we access through our senses and experience, the unconscious requires another way of knowing. Also known since ancient

---

[41] Ibid., 6–7.

[42] Carl G. Jung, *Memories, Dreams, Reflections* (New York: Vintage Books, 1989 <1961>).

[43] Harrell, *Imaginal Figures In Everyday Life,* 8.

[44] Kelly Bulkeley, *Big Dreams: The Science of Dreaming and the Origins of Religion* (New York: Oxford University Press, 2016), 28.

times as gnosis by the Greek world, it is distinguished from the kind of knowledge that comes from intellect and reason alone. "Big dreams are products of the brain working at peak levels of imaginative power and integration."[45] One of the analysts, James Hollis, writes:

> So great is the power of the individual human soul that sooner or later it exercises a profound statement in all our lives. The only matter over which we have a measure of control is whether we can mobilize the courage to take it seriously, establish a dialogue with it, and live in account-ability to the soul in this present world.[46]

Jungian and other depth psychologists warn us that if we fail to recognize and have a dialogue with the forces and complexes in the depths of our personal unconscious and what we inevitably will tap into in the collective unconscious, we sooner or later will encounter these forces in the outer world through our projection.

Archetypes

Archetypes were understood by Jung as formative principles in the unconscious that animate and condition our life experience.[47] The fundamental forms of the archetypes are transcendental in that they are essentially unknowable, lying beyond the limits of the psyche. In the wholeness model, the archetypal forms in the bedrock constellate in the middle as emotion and drives; on the surface they take form as symbols. They appear as the anima or animus (the inner ideal feminine and masculine), the wise old man or woman (the archetype of meaning), the child, the trickster, the hero, rebirth, and the self.[48] The archetypes are universal determinants but they are affected by the cultural

---

[45] Ibid., 271.

[46] James Hollis, *Haunting: Dispelling the Ghosts Who Run Our Lives* (Asheville, NC: Chiron Publications, 2013), 113.

[47] Keiron Le Grice, *Archetypal Reflection: Insights and Ideas from Jungian Psychology* (New York: Muswell Hill Press, 2016), 23.

[48] Ibid., 26.

context (surface) and by the personal experience and personality of the individual,

Le Grice sums up Jung's understanding of archetypes as

not merely static images, but dynamisms, comprising a system of responses based on repeated experience "deposited" in the collective unconscious during evolution, a system of innate responses laid down through the ages.... Archetypes are the pathways or "riverbeds" through which libido or life energy is channeled and flows.[49]

Harrell says that in all imaginal experiences there exists a constellation of affects and beliefs, as well as excitement by at least one archetype, accompanying and contributing to the encounter. These contributing elements allow a "mining" of the experiences, as well as a gathering of knowledge about how the archetype is manifested.[50] Love-Energy is the essential archetype of the soul.[51]

Synchronicity

Jung used his psychological understanding to formulate notions of causality different from classical physics. Seeing a profound interconnectedness of all things, Jung saw patterns of the whole that linked disparate elements unto a unity. He developed this understanding into a theory of synchronicity, a strong metaphor for describing how "disparate elements without apparent connection are brought together or juxtaposed in a manner that tends to shock or surprise the mind, rendering it open to new possibilities, for a broadening of the view of the world, offering a glimpse of the interconnected fabric of the universe."[52]

---

[49] Ibid., 27.

[50] Harrell, *Imaginal Figures In Everyday Life*, 11.

[51] Francis Rothluebber, *Who Creates the Future: Discovering the Essential Energy of Co-Creation* (Lawrenceville, NJ: Womanspace, 2016), 95.

[52] Joseph Cambray, *Synchronicity: Nature and Psyche in an Interconnected Universe* (College Station, TX: Texas A&M University Press, 2009), 31.

Jung defines synchronicity as "a coincidence in time of two or more unrelated events which have the same or a similar meaning. . . . Synchronicity is the unseen process by which humans share, through time and across cultures, common meaningful understandings about life, the universe and the Divine."[53]

The recognition of synchronicity takes us to the bedrock, where ego no longer rules, to a place of deep mutuality.

The Model of Wholeness

We know that electrons are neither waves nor particles but rather something far more nuanced. While they can appear in wave-like and particle-like states, they can also be in infinitely many other states that are neither particle-like nor wave-like. This means that we do not have to split our view of reality into material, mental, or spiritual parts. They are all one. We make distinctions in order to make empirical statements. In so doing we ignore the wholeness, the interconnection of all things.

But reality is even more elusive than that. As the quantum theorists have revealed, our sense of space and time are human centric. Space and time are not relevant at the quantum level. We impose our notions of space and time on everything short of the whole.

Our world is divided, but in our cosmic roots we are already one. Learning from nature about how life depends on the unified reality of the quantum bedrock and learning from the wisdom of mystical religion can inspire us to "create a unified world . . . an evolution toward unity."[54] Catholicity describes the whole-making work of Jesus to bring "people together—physically, emotionally, and spiritually—and healing them of their divisions."[55] In the natural systems of our environment there is both a simplicity and complexity that is dissolved with catholicity.

---

[53] Matthew Fox, *Meister Eckhart: A Mystic Warrior For Our Times* (Novato, CA: New World Library, 2014), 121.

[54] Delio, *Making All Things New*, xxi.

[55] Ilia Delio, *The Emergent Christ: Exploring the Meaning of Catholic in an Evolutionary Universe* (Maryknoll, NY: Orbis Books, 2011), 64.

Body	Mind	Soul
Surface Cells Brain Heart	Symbols Language Thought Ideas	Religion Morality Justice Cataphatic Divinity
Middle Chemical reactions Liquids Gases	Exteriors Feelings Images Dreams	Prayer Meditation Sense of Divine Presence
	--- THE EDGE ---	
Bedrock Waves of Possibility Quantum Particles	Wisdom Intuition Unconscious (personal and collective)	God's Transcendent Love-energy Light of God Limitless Possibility
Core Chaos Uncertainty Randomness	No thought Silence	Darkness Nothingness Emptiness Apophatic Divinity

Figure 1–3. Model of Wholeness

It is the attraction of the whole that has set everything in motion in me, has animated and given organic form to everything. It is because I feel the whole and love it passionately that I believe in the primacy of being. . . . Nothing in the world is intelligible except in and starting from the whole.[56]

With knowledge that reality is one and that making distinctions among body, mind, and soul is arbitrary, I propose the model of wholeness as a method, a tool, to explore the connectedness and possible integration of everything.

The model, based on the quantum biology depiction of life has three dimensions—body, mind, and soul (see Figure 1–3). The three dimensions are portrayed in the three columns. The strata of surface, middle, and bedrock of reality constitute the

---

[56] Pierre Teilhard de Chardin, *Science and Christ* (New York: Harper and Row, 1965), 44.

rows. The core at the bottom of the model represents speculation about what existed before the appearance of quantum particles, consciousness, and even divine presence.

The nine cells (the intersections of the columns and rows) in the model contain a few of the words that describe each dimension-stratum nexus. For example, the surface stratum of the body dimension includes the cells and organs in our bodies.

Chapter 2 provides a detailed description of the content of each stratum and the core with examples from the body, mind, and soul dimensions.

The model shows the potential interconnection of the strata—from the surface down through the middle thermodynamic stratum, down to the quantum bedrock and return. In Chapter 3 I picture this as a cycle and spiral of progression through a web of relationships of bits of information that we put together. We pick up information in each stratum and synthesize it to construct the reality around us and create stories that give a coherent meaning to life.

The biodiversity of the earth, the human mind and emotions, and the biochemical processes cannot be understood in terms of simple laws. The cycling is a complex system that cannot be reduced to its many parts. The emergent behavior is unpredictable and irreducible because the interaction of the parts can produce an infinite number of patterns. The human mind, for example, with the interaction of billions of neurons, cannot be predicted.

"As Holism is a process of creative synthesis, the resulting wholes are not static but dynamic, evolutionary, creative. Hence, evolution has an ever-deepening inward spiritual holistic character" that is moving us toward what we understand as wholeness.[57] However, responding to societal pressure, we often adopt consensus patterns and form our perceptions continually from those patterns.[58]

> Perceptions are thus formed moment by moment as the brain constantly scans the bands of frequencies that surround us; yet, we are often unaware that we are filtering

---

[57] Jan Smuts, *Holism and Evolution* (Sherman Oaks, CA: Sierra Sunrise Publishing, 1999), 87.

[58] Delio, *Making All Things New*, 68.

from a limited set of perceptual patterns. However, if this pattern-recognition behavior does not evolve over time, our perceptual development is in danger of becoming stalled. The result is that we become fixed—or trapped—within a particular reality.[59]

To understand the patterns that emerge from the cycling, we need to use the tools of non-linear complexity science that can describe (not explain) what emerges from the cooperation of a system's many parts. What emerges is our perception of reality. "The 'truths' that we so admire are simply approximations to what is really going on."[60] Cycling helps us to periodically break our perception of reality.

Following McFadden and Al-Khalili, I identify an "edge" between the middle and bedrock strata. This is consistent with how they describe life on the edge of quantum reality. Life at the surface would not exist without the linkage to the bedrock and the ability of living cells to "dance" with the turbulence at the middle. The significance of the "edge" and dancing with the turbulence of the middle for the mind and soul dimensions will be explained in Chapter 3.

The model shows that matter at the surface, whether body (for example, heart beats), the constructions of human consciousness (such as language and symbols), or visible outcroppings of soul (for example, scriptures or houses of worship) are the exterior dimensions of a very dynamic interiority, one that is filled with thermodynamic turbulence, emotions and thoughts, and prayer and meditation. Wholeness heals the split among body, mind, and soul—the three dimensions of one reality.

I also indicate a permeable boundary between the bedrock and the core, which is not included in the quantum biology model. The core originated by currently unknown means—perhaps the Big Bang, wave functions in quantum fields, or a supernatural presence. I speculate more about the core in Chapter 2.

The model has a transformative aspect. Rather than emphasizing wholeness in abstract forms, the model encourages a more

---

[59] Ibid.

[60] Marcel Gleiser, "Making Sense of an Imperfect World," NPR blog 13.7 (March 11, 2010).

imagistic concept. We can picture the dimension and stratum in the wholeness model and reflect on where we are at any given moment. Am I stuck on focusing on the pain in my knee (middle stratum of the body dimension)? Am I overly concerned about what I have said to my neighbor (surface stratum of the mind dimension)? Am I intentionally aware of the divinity of a bird's feather (bedrock stratum of the soul dimension)?

Operationally, the model suggests that to reach higher levels of development as humans, we need to access all nine cells in the model as well as the core.

Conclusion

Bernard Haisch believes that "as biology becomes the most prominent among the sciences, the conception of what it means to be 'scientific' will change. . . . Physics has been successful because it deals with simple, inanimate things for which it is relatively easy to construct and test hypotheses and theories."[61] In biology, emergent properties come forth in more complex systems that operate with unknown laws. The belief in repeatability, reductionism, and the scientific method itself is threatened because carefully controlled tests are difficult in biology.[62]

Haisch relates a story about a biologist

who had made a major discovery in the field involving strains of yeast. He was aghast when his experiment appeared to not be repeatable at another university. . . . After months of nerve-racking mental and laboratory efforts, it was realized that the yeast had mutated as it was moved from one university to another.[63]

As biology becomes more prominent, the issues of consciousness and the mysterious behavior at the quantum level for the existence of life (which metaphorically I am likening to the activity of mind and soul) will raise further questions about our assumptions about reality.

---

[61] Haisch, *The Purpose-Guided Universe*, 176.
[62] Ibid., 177.
[63] Ibid.

Some biologists are considering that the interdependence of living entities is more than independent objects influencing each other by mutual interaction. In this conception, there are "no gaps between subjects and reality independent of the experience of such.[64] The fundamental units of biology are relationships, not the self. For example, an individual tree is a temporary manifestation of a relationship with everything that supports the forest ecosystem.[65] This is consistent with the quantum biology perspective.

Haisch concludes this about reality:

> Does it consist solely of particles and force fields, or is there "real reality" beyond the current domains of physics? Are there phenomena that have no bottom up explanation, even things, like consciousness, that may be far more important ultimately than the discoveries of atom-smashers?[66]

The line between physical life, consciousness, and spirit is not a line at all. The essence of reality is energy flow and information. All things—no matter how great their mass or how hard or solid they appear—are ultimately relationships of living energy and patterns of information.

> Apprehend God in all things
> For God is in all things.
> Every single creature is full of God
> and is a book about God.
> If I spent enough time with the tiniest crea-
>   ture—even a caterpillar—I would never
>   have to prepare a sermon.
> So full of God is every creature.[67]

---

[64] Kriti Sharma, *Interdependence: Biology and Beyond* (New York: Fordham University Press, 2015), 99.

[65] David George Haskell, *The Songs of Trees: Stories from Nature's Great Connectors* (New York: Viking, 2017).

[66] Haisch, *The Purpose-Guided Universe*, 179.

[67] *Meditations with Meister Eckhart: A Centering Book by Matthew Fox* (Rochester, VT: Bear and Co., 1983), 14.

To embrace fully the potential of what we are learning from quantum biologists and the model of wholeness to explain the One Reality, we need both faith in what science has revealed and a creative imagination about what may be possible as revealed by religion. But most important, as suggested by the following poem by William Wallace, is our sense of wonder and mystery that aids us "to stop and pause."

When Our World of Thought Lies Shattered

When our world of thought lies shattered
As its truths fragment and die
We will trust the mystery's oneness
Held within the Earth and sky.
What we once conceived as solid
We now know is full of space,
What seems static and unmoving
Science shows is not the case.
All we thought was unconnected
Now is linked with cosmic thread.
What was seen as unrelated
Genes unite as one instead.
Faith that claims to be rock-solid
Holds some parts but not the whole.
Only through the Spirit's flowing
Can we find our journey's goal.
Can our faith survive this turmoil?
Can it reverence newfound laws?
Yes, when wonder is our helpmate
Aiding us to stop and pause.
Glory be for sacred mystery.
Praise for all life's wondrous ways.
Celebrate emerging knowledge
Woven in a ring of praise.[68]

---

[68] William L. (Bill) Wallace, "When Our World of Thought Lies Shattered," *The Boundless Life Collection* (New Zealand: Methodist Church of New Zealand, 2014).

Chapter 2

The Strata of Wholeness

As we explore the dimensions of body, mind, and soul, we find multiple fields of experience that parallel what quantum biologists call strata.

We use our senses and analytic capability (for example, logic) to engage the three-dimensional physical world on the surface stratum. The surface is the context of what is around us—the forces, conditions, structures, and worldviews that contain what is happening, that frame it and give it meaning.

We engage our feelings and emotions in the middle stratum to make judgments about what we have encountered on the surface.

We engage our imagination and intuition to gain a deeper, holistic understanding at the bedrock stratum.

All three strata provide awareness, resourcefulness, motivation, and wisdom. Wholeness emerges from the relationships of these strata.

As we traverse these strata, our experiences of time may be linear or cyclical. Sometimes we have intimations of timelessness and "drop into a fertile stillness that words cannot describe . . . a sense of isolation . . . a sense of connectedness and oneness with all of creation" at the core.[1]

In this chapter I explore the similarity of what we experience in each stratum of the three dimensions. For example, at the surface our experiences are material, tangible, and logical.

---

[1] James Reho, *Tantric Jesus: The Erotic Heart of Early Christianity* (Rochester, VT: Destiny Books, 2017), 18.

At the middle stratum, we experience turbulence and fluidity of liquids, gases, emotion, and yearnings. At the bedrock, there is a realm of possibility and love. At times it is difficult to know what stratum is affecting our experience. In the soul dimension, for example, when in church, the physical trappings and ambience (surface) may put us into a meditative state. Or our feelings (middle) about a recent loss may put us in a pensive mood. Or, we intuit (bedrock) the presence of the Divine. Or, it could be all three strata that move us to pray.

We usually attribute our experience to only one of the dimensions to make distinctions, but our experience is affected by all three dimensions. Our experience of joy is likely to be physical, mental, and spiritual at the same moment in time.

Although I distinguish among the contents of the dimensions, my focus on the wholeness of the dimensions of body, mind, and soul also pertains to distinctions among the three strata and the core. There is a thin line between what we experience in the material, tangible, reality of facts and reason in life on the surface and the feelings, emotions, turbulence, ideas, and images in the middle. Even moving to the dreams and possibilities of the bedrock can be a thin line. If something on the surface strikes us as mysterious and unknown, it can instantly trigger our emotions and stir our unconscious at the bedrock, which is where we interface with archetypal forces beyond our control. Likewise, if an archetype manifests in our dreams, it can trigger emotions and drivers in the middle that affect what we do on the surface.

On July 4, 2016, I had the following dream:

> I am swimming in a lake when I notice a family setting up a picnic at the bottom of the lake. It was the same configuration they had on the shore (surface) but they moved it to the lake bottom (bedrock). I swam, going from the shallow to the deep water, and back to the shore. I was thinking about the seasons where swimming was possible.

As I reflect on the picnic experiences in my life, I am reminded of the joy about being outside enjoying the spring after a hard Minnesota winter. In my dreams I have occasionally experienced the same joy.

The dream suggests that the reality I experience on the surface is similar at the bedrock. All the patterns, structures, and behaviors I create at the surface exist as possibilities in the bedrock. It also suggests that I can go to the bedrock to find a reality I can then replicate on the surface.

The three strata and the core provide a way to understand the levels of meditation and contemplation experienced and taught by mystics through the ages. Evelyn Underhill, a historian of mystical practices, masterfully summarized three levels of contemplation of reality:

- The *Natural World of Becoming*—the discovery of God in creation (surface and middle).
- The *Metaphysical World of Being*—the apprehension of infinite Reality in what is finite (bedrock).
- The *Divine Reality*—trustful dwelling in God (the core).[2]

Although the three levels of contemplation are woven together, Underhill recommends beginning with the natural world, which in the wholeness model is similar to the surface and middle strata as they involve both thinking and emotion. When we can quiet our thoughts and feelings, we can enter Underhill's second level, the metaphysical world of being that I call the bedrock. In the bedrock we enter the realm of our intuitions, dreams, and capacity to love. As we deepen our contemplation we enter Underhill's third level, which I call the core, the source of everything.

For example, on the surface our ego experiences conflict and greed. If we descend to the core we can experience the ground of our being (God) that guides us up to the bedrock of possibilities, up through the turbulent middle stratum and finally to our life on the surface where we can let go of our ego's need to control and dominate.

What is resolved or unresolved in us at the lower strata will drive our action at the surface. When we seek our deepest self in the core and bedrock, we find the answer to what troubles us and what is the highest good for an evolving world.

---

[2] Evelyn Underhill, *Practical Mysticism* (New York: Dutton, 1914), 85–122.

As I describe each stratum and the core in the wholeness model, I blend Underhill's description with my understanding of the strata as described in quantum biology, consciousness studies, and contemporary spiritual practice.

In Chapter 3 we cycle through the strata in each of the three dimensions of body, mind, and soul.

Surface Stratum

The surface is the material reality we experience. At the surface we see and experience beauty and order of the planets, stars, and galaxies we behold in the evening sky. It is also where we see and experience the trains, planes, and skyscrapers we have created. At the surface we make resolutions to achieve our goals, express our compassion for others, and take actions to transform the world. In this tangible reality we are recognized, have communion with, and are valued by others. Here is where we exercise power, read, listen, taste, touch, see, and love one another. The surface is where we encounter strangers who can teach us new things.

In the *body* dimension we experience the surface as our biosphere—the material surface of the earth occupied by living organisms. The cells in our bodies take advantage of some self-organizing properties that create life. We experience the fire, air, water, and soil of the earth.

In the *mind* dimension we have a consciousness that weaves symbols, language, and icons into patterns of meaning. We have memories of specific times, spaces and events. We reason, calculate, and decide about what to do on the surface.

In the *soul* dimension we have a sense of being a spiritual being. We develop tenets of justice, codes of ethics and morality, and creeds. We give expression to these aspects in our religious and spiritual rituals and practices.

Engagement with God in the multiplicity of forms of the natural order of creation is the first of Underhill's three ways of contemplation. Persons can opt to bring a high degree of conscious awareness to their engagement of the created order or not.[3] Underhill says that engaging the natural world is about

---

[3] Colleen M. Griffith, "Underhill's Practical Mysticism: One Hundred Years Later," *NTR* 27, no. 1 (September 2014).

loving and patient exploration, finding the self-expression of that Immanent Being in every manifestation of life.[4]

> Stretch out by a distinct act of loving will towards one of the myriad manifestations of life that surround you. . . . Pour yourself out towards it, do not draw its image towards you. Deliberate—more impassioned-attentiveness, an attentiveness which soon transcends all consciousness of yourself. . . .
>
> As to the object of contemplation, it matters little. . . . Anything will do, provided that your attitude be right: for all things in this world towards which you are stretching out are linked together, and one truly apprehended will be the gateway to the rest.[5]

In this first way of contemplation Underhill points out that attentiveness to everything around us will begin to take us deeper into the world. We transcend consciousness of our self as we contemplate the song of a bird, the taste of fresh spring water, a picture of our loved one, or a passage from scripture. Any surface aspect of the body, mind, and soul dimensions can give voice to a sacred reality.

Culture

We can best understand the surface dimension if we consider the civilizations and cultures we have created to buffer us from nature. Some, like the aboriginal cultures, evolved and adapted to nature. Others, like the industrial culture, set themselves apart from nature and created worldviews that produce consequences inimical to long-term survival (e.g. climate change, overpopulation, pollution, and famine).

Jonathon Marks, a professor of anthropology at the University of North Carolina (Charlotte), says that the cultures we construct are essentially imagery worlds:

> Like the imaginary connection between your fingertip and the object you are pointing at, humans inhabit a largely

---

[4] Underhill, *Practical Mysticism*, 51.
[5] Ibid., 52.

imagery world—one of law, marriage, political inequality, aesthetics, morality, and hope. . . . Culture is a make-believe world, a fantasy, a bunch of rules that we are born into, and which end up structuring and giving meaning to our lives.[6]

The civilizations that humans have constructed do widen the possibilities and opportunities and new choices for the next generation. Now, with the flood of digital technology, we have developed a global civilization. The challenge is to recognize which cultural constructs, rules, and structures are no longer adapted to our survival, and which cultural artifacts still provide value and significance.

David Brooks, the noted *New York Times* columnist, regularly points out cultural shortcomings in our current era of aging population, telecommuting workers, single-parent households, and the culture and geography of suburbia that are failing to nurture webs of mutual interdependence. "They are successful people who worked hard and built good lives but who are left nonetheless strangely isolated, in attenuated communities, and who are left radiating the residual sadness of the lonely heart."[7]

The major problem in finding meaning on the surface is that our attachment to objects, processes, or doctrines can become idolatrous. Regarding our attachment to social media: How many times do we check our email or go on Twitter or Facebook in a day? Consider this test for whether something is idolatrous: If you lose it, will you feel anxious and fearful about your self-identity?

Scriptures can become idols if they do not speak to the realities of our life and what we know to be true, particularly if we read them only literally or overanalyze them until the mystery and beauty are destroyed.

Even so, when we contemplate and participate in the deeper levels of reality below the surface, we have a connection to the

---

[6] Jonathan Marks, "What of the Human Mind Evolved for Non-rational Thought? An Anthropological Perspective" (paper presented at the Institute for Religion and Science, Star Island, NH, 2016).

[7] David Brooks, "An Economic Survival Story," *New York Times* (September 20, 2016).

whole. Encounters with mystery on the surface can part the thin veil between the ordinary of our lives on the surface and the divine light that is within everything.

Interaction of the Three Dimensions at the Surface

The three dimensions of body, mind, and soul are intertwined at the surface. Some examples of how we experience this wholeness in our everyday lives are the following:

body ↔ mind

When our ancestors encountered the bison and horses in the natural world they realized that the animals had a spirit they wanted to represent in their cave paintings.

body ↔ soul

Our ancestors observed patterns in the heavens and created sun gods and constellations that provided solace and comfort to troubled souls. Icons serve as a timeless doorway to communion with the Divine on the surface.

mind ↔ soul

Our spiritual practices influence the civic culture. For example, the Ten Commandments of the Judaic-Christian tradition have influenced many cultures in the world.

 body ↔ mind ↔ soul

The interaction of our physical needs, our mental constructs, and our religious practices have created distinct and competitive tribes, communities, and nation states. This interaction also makes possible cooperation and the pursuit of common interests.

Middle Stratum

In her description of the first meditation—the discovery of God in creation—Underhill uses language that describes the turbulent and exciting middle stratum.

By this quiet yet tense act of communion, this loving gaze, you will presently discover a relationship—far more intimate than anything you imagined—between yourself and the surrounding "objects of sense."

A subtle interpenetration of your spirit with the spirit of those "unseen existences," now so deeply and thrillingly felt by you, will take place. Old barriers will vanish. . . .

Humility and awe will be evoked in you by the beautiful and patient figures of the poor. . . . [You will] feel them as infinitely significant and adorable parts of the Transcendent Whole in which you also are immersed. . . .

This experience will be, in the very highest sense, the experience of sensation without thought.[8]

Underhill is describing the necessity to choose deep awareness on the surface to participate in an animated, sensate world in the middle stratum. Everything is sacred.

Body Dimension

The middle stratum of the body dimension is the turbulent dynamic physical world of gases, liquids, and metabolism. As we saw in Chapter 1, our cells need to "dance" with this turbulence to maintain a connection to bedrock coherence.

When we consider that the brain has 10 billion neurons cells generating 10^{18} operations at once, we know that it is more than a super computer. These operations are intelligent quantum waves that are simultaneously processing billions of bits of information. The turbulence in the brain is matched by the turbulence in our body's cells. As we grow and develop, the biological field of epigenetics shows that carefully orchestrated chemical reactions activate and deactivate parts of the genome at strategic times and in specific locations. The field of epigenetics explores how external factors such as the environment can change how genetic information is used and inherited without alterations in the DNA sequence.

---

[8] Underhill, *Practical Mysticism*, 53–55.

Epigenetic change is a regular and natural occurrence but can also be influenced by several factors including age, the environment/lifestyle, and disease state. Epigenetic modifications can manifest as commonly as the manner in which cells terminally differentiate to end up as skin cells, liver cells, brain cells, etc. Or, epigenetic change can have more damaging effects that can result in diseases like cancer.[9]

The environment, individual lifestyles, and our attitudes can also directly interact with the genome to influence epigenetic change. These changes may be reflected at various stages throughout a person's life and even in later generations, allowing organisms to respond to environmental changes rapidly and effectively.

The turbulent activity in the brain, the impact of the environment, and our own ability to affect the physical changes in the middle stratum indicate how the meditation described by Underhill requires a focus on our physical being—our breathing, our diet, and our patterns of exercise. For example, a yogi can choose to control respiration by stopping breathing as long as possible between exhaling and inhaling. The flow of thoughts, sensations, images that courses through the mind are concentrated on one point. By repressing the memories and associations with these thoughts, sensation and images, the yogi sees them through a filter of wholeness.

Mind Dimension

In the mind dimension the middle is the realm of our ideas, thoughts, passions, images, and emotions that fuel our wonder and behavior on the surface. Feelings of optimism, humility, daring, courage, love, and compassion propel us into living a virtuous life. Our inner ideas, thoughts, and emotions also fuel our cynicism, our apathy, despair, partisanship, cowardice, nostalgia, fear, shame, and indifference. In the mind dimension we experience the turbulence in the middle stratum in a range of

---

[9] G. Egger et al., "Epigenetics in Human Disease and Prospects for Epigenetic Therapy," *Nature* (2004), 429, 457–63.

emotions that connect and commit to what we each find to be most meaningful.

The middle is also where we actively contemplate the future. Using our intuitive powers, we can lift our spirits or become depressed and anxious, whether we are assessing our own lives or worrying about the nation. "The main purpose of emotions is to guide future behavior and moral judgments, according to researchers in a new field called prospective psychology. Emotions enable you to empathize with others by predicting their behavior."[10]

Consultants to the Pixar movie "Inside Out" identified five emotions that define our identities. They are enjoyment (joy), fear, anger, disgust, and sadness. From their study of the science of emotion they conclude that emotions organize—rather than disrupt—rational thinking and our social lives. For example, "when we are angry we are acutely attuned to what is unfair, which helps animate actions that remedy injustice. . . . Expression of embarrassment triggers others to forgive when we've acted in ways that momentarily violate social norms." If we embrace sadness and let it unfold, "sadness will clarify what has been lost" and move us toward what is to be gained.[11]

In many nonhuman mammals, goose bumps—that physiological reaction in which the muscles surrounding hair follicles contract—occur when individuals, along with other members of their species, face a threat. We humans, by contrast, can get goose bumps when we experience awe, that often-positive feeling of being in the presence of something vast that transcends our understanding of the world.[12]

Awe is an emergent or meta-emotion that "motivates people to do things that enhance the greater good. Awe . . . leads people

---

[10] Martin E. P. Seligman and John Tierney, "We Aren't Built to Live in the Moment," *New York Times*, May 21, 2017.

[11] Dacher Keltner and Paul Ekman, "The Science of 'Inside Out,'" *New York Times*, July 3, 2015.

[12] Paul Piff and Dacher Keltner, "Why Do We Experience Awe?" *New York Times*, May 22, 2015, SR10.

to feel less narcissistic and entitled and more attuned to the common humanity people share with one another."[13]

In terms of the wholeness model, awesome experiences on the surface drive people to the middle, where they experience positive emotions of wonder and beauty, and further down to the bedrock, where they feel love and connection to their surroundings, including the people around them.

The implication is that we need to experience more awe daily by pursuing what gives us goose bumps. Looking at the stars or seeing butterflies in bushes is awesome, even sacred.

The middle stratum can be viewed as the locus of the irrational. Matthew Fox lists what Otto Rank, a psychoanalyst, categorized as irrational:

Dreams, music, dance, art, ritual, sex, love-making, babies, laughter, play, massage, drumming, singing, the smell of newly cut grass, the tastes of spicy foods, silence, grief, color, creativity, peace, clowning, nature, wilderness, prayer, fear, animals, angels or spirits, children, beauty, paradox, myth, stories, games, campfires, chant, darkness, tenderness, forgiveness, meditation, God, birds, trees, plants, flowers, and food. And, Rank adds, "legitimate foolishness," the folly that accompanies wisdom. Holy folly.[14]

Fox then exclaims: "What would life be without these?" The irrational aspects of our lives, those aspects without reason, give us "reasons for living, the zest for carrying on."[15]

Our challenge is to explore the truth about our troubling past thoughts and emotions to set us free from stress and pain.

Soul Dimension

In the soul dimension we strive for experiences that open the heart in a way that offers both bliss and a deep sense of

---

[13] Ibid.

[14] Matthew Fox, *Meister Eckhart: A Mystic Warrior for Our Times* (Novato, CA: New World Library, 2014), 141.

[15] Ibid.

connection and ecstatic identity through prayer and meditation, active imagination, encounter with nature, or gazing at the stars.

Our focus in the soul dimension is not on a God that is elsewhere, a God that is waiting to hear our petitions about what we need or even what our dear friends need. The focus is on identifying and clearing away what is happening in the middle strata that keeps us from accessing the grace and wisdom at the bedrock. There we may find answers to what troubles us and what we long for.

For example, repentance is being honest with yourself about who you really are—all of your longings and aspirations. Douglas Christie writes about the Christian monastic tradition, where tears were seen as an indication that the heart was breaking open.

> For the monks, the meaning of these tears was often very ambiguous. There was sadness and regret around the awareness of your complicity in having caused suffering for yourself and others, but there was also something close to joy. The relief of tears signified a dam bursting, an opening up of the soul to stand more honestly in relation to reality.[16]

The "tears signified a dam bursting, an opening up of the soul" that describes how the turbulence in the middle stratum is often a gateway to the bedrock.

We usually think of the Lord's Prayer as a petition for daily bread, forgiveness, and deliverance. A version of the Lord's Prayer by Paul Laughlin helps see the soul dimension as the seat of our deep feelings:

> O presence and pow'r within us,
> being and light of all.
> How we are filled,
> how we 'erflow
> with infinite love and gladness!

---

[16] Garrison Institute, "Toward a Contemplative Ecology: A Conversation with Douglas Christie and Andrew Zolli" (2017), https://www.garrisoninstitute.org/blog/toward-contemplative-ecology/.

We shall this day sow grace and peace,
and show mercy to all,
and gentle loving kindness.
And we shall not be so self-serving,
but a constant source of giving.
For ours is the essence,
and the wholeness,
and the fullness
forever.
Amen.[17]

Prayer like this fills us with positive emotions of love and gladness and kindness to all. These emotions are a gateway to the coherence in the bedrock where we can find what is true, beautiful, and good. We also find love. We are in the heart of God, which is the gateway to the core, the unfathomable Source of everything we might wish for.

Interaction of the Three Dimensions in the Middle Strata

At the middle, when the three dimensions interact, our ideas, images, moments, occasions, sounds, and music form into meaningful patterns.

body ↔ mind

The chemical mix in our bodies influences our emotions, endocrine systems, and dreams. The production of endorphins and secretions of the pituitary and pineal glands through physical exercise create a good mood. Conversely, if we are depressed or agitated, including nightmares, our blood pressure can rise and our bodies are stressed. We create symbols and metaphors to express our bodily experience, for example, "I have a gut feeling."

body ↔ soul

When we are stressed, ensuring our bodies have sufficient sleep, good nutrition, and exercise increases our capacity for

---

[17] Paul Allen Laughlin, "Pray without Seeking: Towards a Truly Mystical Lord's Prayer: Part Two," *The Fourth R* 22, no. 6 (November-December 2009), 20–23.

prayer and meditation. Because meditation and prayer have a calming effect on our bodily processes, our sense of stress is reduced.

mind ↔ soul

Our emotional state, including recurring images and dreams, intrudes into prayer and meditation and affects our sense of God's presence. When we go into a deep prayer, such as in a retreat, the quality of our emotions and dreams is positively influenced.

body ↔ mind ↔ soul

Music operates in the middle stratum in all three dimensions. Our brains have "neural pathways that react almost exclusively to the sound of music—any music. . . . When a musical passage is played, a distinct set of neurons tucked inside a furrow of a listener's auditory cortex will fire in response. Other sounds, by contrast—a dog barking, a car skidding, a toilet flushing—leave the musical circuits unmoved."[18] Scientists believe that music making was important in developing group cohesion in early human development.

In the middle, our bodily, mental, and spiritual experiences together create powerful reactions as we have communion with others and nature. This is illustrated by the following story by Alan Lightman, a novelist and an MIT physicist. The story captures the dynamic interaction of all three dimensions at the middle stratum.

A family of ospreys lived in a large nest near his summer home in Maine. In mid-April, the parents would arrive from South America and lay eggs and raise their babies until the fledglings took their first flight in late summer. Lightman and his wife recorded these cycles of life every year in their "osprey journals."

> Then, one August afternoon, the two baby ospreys of that season took flight for the first time as I stood on the circular deck of my house watching the nest. All summer long, they had watched me on that deck as I watched

---

[18] Natalie Angier, "New Ways into the Brain's 'Music Room,'" *New York Times*, February 8, 2016, D2.

them. To them, it must have looked like I was in my nest just as they were in theirs. On this particular afternoon, their maiden flight, they did a loop of my house and then headed straight at me with tremendous speed. My immediate impulse was to run for cover, since they could have ripped me apart with their powerful talons. But something held me to my ground. When they were within 20 feet of me, they suddenly veered upward and away. But before that dazzling and frightening vertical climb, for about half a second we made eye contact. Words cannot convey what was exchanged between us in that instant. It was a look of connectedness, of mutual respect, of recognition that we shared the same land. After they were gone, I found that I was shaking, and in tears. To this day, I cannot explain what happened in that half-second. But it was one of the most profound moments of my life.[19]

At that moment both Lightman and the osprey could have experienced this event as the acknowledgment of the other. This is a good example of coherence of the three dimensions and three strata.

Bedrock Stratum

Bedrock connotes firmness, certainty, stability—all of which are "opposite" of what is intended. Bedrock is about essence, genesis, and emergent possibilities.

Body Dimension

To explore the bedrock in the body dimension, let's start with a rock.

Depending on the rock's size it could contain 1,000 trillion trillion atoms. The electrons and smaller particles in the atoms—protons and neutrons—are composed of quarks. Understanding a rock requires consideration of only a few aspects. The forces

---

[19] Alan Lightman, "Does God Exist?" In Salon.com-Life, October 2, 2011.

that govern the interaction of the particles in the rock's atoms are well known. Electrons, protons, neutrons, and gluons give the rock its form and bulk.

The jostling and constant interaction of the atoms in rocks and other solids and liquids keep the atoms in an incoherent state, thus providing the stability and predictability we count on in everyday life. We don't expect that a rock in our garden or the table we are eating on will disassemble or transform.

In the case of living cells, however, the atomic particles such as protons are engaged in a choreographed "dance."[20] The vibrating motion of the "dance" brings atoms and molecules into close enough proximity to allow their particles (electrons and protons) to quantum tunnel.[21]

> The discovery that enzymes in the cells promote the dematerialization of particles from one part in space and their instantaneous materialization in another provides us with a novel insight into the mystery of life. . . . Life takes special measures to capture advantages provided by the quantum world to make its cells work.[22]

The life of the cells at the surface is linked to the particles in the atoms in the bedrock. What influences this linkage is still mostly a mystery, but what happens in the bedrock stratum is the foundation of what happens on the surface. The bedrock is like a pool of shimmering water, waiting, to which our living cells must connect.

Mind Dimension

In January 2017 I had a dream in which the following statement appeared: *Yert is the inner person.* When I awoke, I had no immediate idea of the meaning of *yert*. I then remembered the round "hippie" homes popular in the 1950s referred to as yerts.

---

[20] Johnjoe McFadden and Jim Al-Khalili, *Life on the Edge: The Coming of Age of Quantum Biology* (New York: Crown Publishers, 2014), 91.

[21] Ibid., 97.

[22] Ibid., 97–98.

On the Internet I found that *yert* is a word or greeting used in Sparta, Tennessee, to indicate one's happiness or approval. I have never been to Sparta, but in my imagination it could be a place like the bedrock, where my innermost mind can be happy and basking in approval and perhaps free, like the hippie lifestyle.[23] In Turkey, *yert* means clan or community or extended family, so it could suggest an inner state of coherence.

In living systems when the atoms are in a coherent state described by quantum biologists, amazing things can happen at the bedrock. Just as hydrogen atoms in our body get into alignment by the powerful magnets in an MRI machine, the aspects of mind at the bedrock can, metaphorically, become aligned and coherent. At the bedrock there is infinite space and time without boundaries. The present, past, and future are one. Consciousness exists in a wave of possibilities and probabilities.

Our small ego self at the surface will often close the coherence available at the bedrock, but if we can quiet our ego, the coherence at the bedrock allows our larger self to emerge on the surface.

David Brooks uses the term *inspiration* to describe what I am calling the coherence at the bedrock:

> When one is inspired, time disappears or alters its pace. The senses are amplified. There may be goose bumps or shivers down the spine, or a sense of being overawed by some beauty.
>
> Inspiration is always more active than mere appreciation. There's a thrilling feeling of elevation, a burst of energy, an awareness of enlarged possibilities. The person in the grip of inspiration has received, as if by magic, some new perception, some holistic understanding, along with the feeling that she is capable of more than she thought. . . .
>
> Most important, inspiration demands a certain posture, the sort of posture people feel when they are overawed by something large and mysterious. They are both humbled

---

[23] In August 2017, while at the Chautauqua Institution in New York, my wife and I learned of a retirement village in Pleasant Hill, Tennessee. We visited and purchased a home there. I then found out that our post office address is Sparta, Tennessee. Quantum weirdness?

and self-confident, surrendering and also powerful. When people are inspired, they are willing to take a daring leap toward something truly great. They're brave enough to embrace the craggy fierceness of the truth and to try to express it in some new way.[24]

Experiencing such inspiration can impel us beyond our anxiety and normal risk avoidance, freeing us to take action on the surface.

Soul Dimension

The mind at the bedrock of the soul is often characterized by light. We experience it as intuition, our way of perceiving reality that is as fast as lightning. *Eureka!* and *flash of insight* are phrases that speak to an instantaneous understanding. I had this recent dream thought: *Light must come from both within and without.*

Carl Jung in *The Red Book* said:

> Do you still not know that the way to truth stands open only to those without intentions? . . . We tie ourselves up with intentions, not mindful of the fact that intention is the limitation, yes, the exclusion of life. We believe that we can eliminate the darkness with an intention, and in that way, aim past the light. How can we presume to know in advance from where the light will come to us?[25]

Jung's reflection suggests that we get in the way of lightning-fast revelations by having intentions that limit us. Or, by having an agenda for others, we aim for enlightenment but miss it because light (insight) comes from the bedrock, which is composed of possibilities, not certainties.

Thomas Merton writes that the light within, the spark, the pure truth, belongs to God. Agreeing with Jung, Merton says we can't access this with intention:

---

[24] David Brooks, "What Is Inspiration?" *New York Times*, April 25, 2016, A27.

[25] C. G. Jung, *The Red Book* (New York: W. W. Norton and Company, 2009), 144.

At the center of our being is a point of nothingness that is untouched by sin and by illusions, a point of pure truth, a point or spark which belongs entirely to God, which is never at our disposal, from which God disposes our lives, which is inaccessible to the fantasies of our mind or the brutalities of our own will. . . . It is like a pure diamond, blazing with the invisible light of heaven. It is in everybody, and if we could see it we would see these billions of points of light coming together in the face and blaze of a sun that would make all the darkness and cruelty of life vanish completely.[26]

In the soul dimension the bedrock is a space where God works compassion and where the love of God is active. At the bedrock, we encounter radiant light, where Christians experience the Christ, the light of the world,[27] or what the Buddhists call enlightenment.

John Philip Newell says that the light of God "burst the Universe into being at the beginning of time and still pulsates at the heart of everything that has been created." It is "a subterranean river running deep in the folds of the universe."[28]

The second form of contemplation for the mind at the bedrock of the soul Underhill describes as:

a steady acquiescence, a simple and loyal surrender to the great currents of life . . . a surrender not limp but deliberate. . . . When, therefore, you put aside your preconceived ideas, your self-centered scale of values, and let intuition have its way with you, you open up by this act new levels of the world. . . . [You] realize that the words and notes which so often puzzled you by displaying an intensity

---

[26] Thomas Merton, *Conjectures of a Guilty Bystander* (New York: Image Classics, 1968), 155.

[27] James Reho alerted me to the Athonite tradition in Christianity—in particular, Gregory of Palamas (fourteenth century), who talked about the experience of the "uncreated light" within the human person.

[28] John Philip Newell, *The Rebirthing of God: Christianity's Struggle for New Beginnings* (Woodstock, VT: Skylight Paths Publishing, 2015), 32–33.

that exceeded the demands of your little world, only have beauty and meaning just because and in so far as you discern them to be the partial expressions of a greater whole which is still beyond your reach.[29]

With Jung and Merton, Underhill sees that accessing the light at the bedrock is beyond our control. The language in her description of the second level of contemplation provides an excellent overview of the spiritual bedrock:

[Your attention] is directed towards a plane of existence with which your bodily senses have no attachments. [You] will find yourself, emptied and freed, in a place stripped bare of all the machinery of thought; and achieve the condition of simplicity. Yet in spite of the darkness that enfolds you, the Cloud of Unknowing into which you have plunged, you are sure that it is well to be here. A peculiar certitude which you cannot analyze, a strange satisfaction and peace, is distilled into you. . . .

Such an experience of Eternity, the attainment of that intuitive awareness . . . which the mystics call . . . the Quiet, the Desert of God, the Divine Dark, represents the utmost that human consciousness can do of itself towards the achievement of union with Reality. [This state of awareness] is of necessity a fleeting experience. . . . Perpetual absorption in the Transcendent is a human impossibility, and the effort to achieve it is both unsocial and silly. But this experience . . . changes forever the proportions of the life that once has known it; gives to it depth and height, and prepares the way for that great transfiguration of existence which comes when the personal activity of the finite will gives place to the great and compelling action of another Power.[30]

Building on Teilhard de Chardin, Cynthia Bourgeault affirms that love is the primary energy in the bedrock of the soul.

---

[29] Underhill, *Practical Mysticism*, 57, 59.
[30] Ibid., 68–69.

Love means the release of yet another quantum packet of that sum total of consciousness and conscience . . . seeded into the cosmos . . . in that initial eclosion of divine yearning that launched the whole journey in the first place.

True union . . . doesn't turn its respective participants into a blob, a drop dissolving in the ocean. Rather, it presses them mightily to become more and more themselves: to discover, trust, and fully inhabit their own depths. As these depths open, so does their capacity to love, to give-and-receive of themselves over the entire range of their actualized personhood.[31]

The Dynamics of Soul

We can only explore the dynamics of the bedrock of the soul by using our creative imagination. Harrell describes the multiple realities as figures and shapes that are unique, ambiguous, changeable, and fluid representations of the self. The figures are autonomous independent beings within the psyche. Our imagination can bring this intuitive content to the surface.[32]

These imaginal figures can help us understand the unconscious domain because they have both aspects of an ego self and aspects of our personal and collective unconscious. They are at the same time irrational and intuitive. In the imaginal realm, figures can appear as part of a vision or in lucid dreams.

Dreams provide guidance, comfort or "truth" from what appears to be a divine presence. These dreams can be so dramatic that they transform a person's life or the course of history (as evidenced from biblical history).

Divine beings that appear in dreams are archetypes, patterns from within the collective unconscious that guide the human psyche toward a state of wholeness. When we encounter these images in the bedrock they can help us to create more balance and wholeness in our lives if we take the time to consider what

---

[31] Cynthia Bourgeault, "Love Is the Answer—What Is the Question?, Omega Center blog, September 12, 2016.

[32] Mary Harrell, *Imaginal Figures In Everyday Life: Stories From the World between Matter and mind* (Asheville, NC: InnerQuest Books, 2015), 5–7.

lessons they are communicating. For men, the divine presence may appear as the Anima, a divine feminine presence that offers guidance. For women, typically the symbol is the Animus, a divine masculine presence.[33] If the divine presence is of the same sex as the dreamer, it may be a shadow figure that is trying to help the dreamer to a higher level of development of the Anima (for women) or Animus (for men).

The shadow figure is likely trying to move the ego closer to the wisdom embodied in the figure.

Sophia (the Greek word for wisdom) is identified in the Wisdom of Solomon as the divine wisdom of God, the creator of the world. She is "all-powerful, overseeing all" and she "pervades and penetrates all things." The author of the Wisdom of Solomon is functionally establishing Sophia as the divine activity.[34]

In the Gospel of John, by calling the preexistent Christ the Logos, John shows that he understands Christ to be the Sophia of God. This is one way to understand the many accounts of visions, encounters, dreams, and appearances of the person of Jesus the Christ throughout history.[35]

Interaction of the Three Dimensions at the Bedrock

Some physicists have recently demonstrated that at the quantum (bedrock) level there is no predefined causal order or predefined time.[36] So, if the movement of atoms and molecules, our mental intuition, and our experience of spirit are happening at the same time, what is cause and what is effect are entangled.

body ↔ mind

Our living cells' dependence on the bedrock of possibilities, where there are almost magical movements of electron and

---

[33] C. G Jung, "Relations between the Ego and the Unconscious," in *The Portable Jung, Part 5*, ed. Joseph Campbell (New York: The Viking Press, 1971), 53–54.

[34] James Reho, *Tantric Jesus: The Erotic Heart of Early Christianity* (Rochester, VT: Destiny Books, 2017).

[35] Phillip H. Wiebe, *Visions and Appearances of Jesus* (Abilene, TX: Leafwood Publishers, 2014).

[36] See Giulia Rubino et al., "Experimental Verification of an Indefinite Causal Order," *Science Advances* 3, no. 3 (August 2016).

photons, may also explain why we have the flashes of insight, the awareness of things our rational minds cannot deduce. Conversely, these intuitions affect our behavior, which can affect the metabolism in our physical bodies.

body ↔ soul

The quantum leaps in our cells are the light of the Spirit that quickens our ability to find divine love in the bedrock. When we tap into the light and love of God, it affects what is happening physically in our bodies—our blood pressure and the linkage of our neurons.

mind ↔ soul

Our heightened awareness pushes us into some of the bigger questions of life: Who am I? Why am I here? Where am I going? When we are filled with the Spirit at the bedrock our boundaries are opened and our horizons are expanded to take in new vistas.

body ↔ mind ↔ soul

When there is coherence in the bedrock in all three dimensions, we become more whole, more attuned to our development as human beings and as expressions of the development of the cosmos. Most of our imaging of the future occurs in the bedrock as the brain sifts information to generate predictions.[37] Our conscious and unconscious minds come together. We develop understanding and desire as we experience the presence of the Divine within.

The Core

Nobel Laureate Frank Wilczek uses the term *core* to cover the mathematical explanation of the quantum fields of subatomic particles, electromagnetism, gravity, the nuclear forces, the Higgs field that give mass to everything, and how everything interacts with light and radiation. The equations provide a firm foundation for all the physical sciences. But the equations don't account

---

[37] Seligman and Tierney, "We Aren't Built to Live in the Moment," 1.

for dark energy and dark matter, which makes up 96 percent of the known universe, or address the possibility that there is a deeper unity that links everything together, including human imagination and calculation.[38] The core is the field of creativity and the fundamental source of all energy and matter for quantum particles that pop in and out of being.

Ervin Laszlo states:

Underlying the manifest three-dimensional world of particles, forces and interaction, there is a world that does not contain energy and matter in the known form, nor does it include space and time in the accepted sense. This deeper basement is the cosmic plenum. It transmits photons and bosons—the wave propagation that we know as light and force—and constitutes the common substrate of all the universes that evolve and devolve in the Metaverse.[39]

A remarkable parallel description of this field of generativity is in the Gospel of John, where the Word of God is described as that through whom all things began. I believe the core in the wholeness model is the source of all the "somethings" in the three dimensions of body, mind, and soul and is also the same as the field of generativity described in John's Gospel.

The earth's molten core creates the earth's magnetic field, which deflects solar wind particles that would blow away our atmosphere. It is speculated that when Mars lost its molten core, the atmosphere dissipated. As an analogy, the core in the wholeness model holds the dimensions and strata together.

Although the second law of thermodynamics says that disorder or entropy increases until it reaches a state of inactivity, research by Wilczek on quantum chromodynamics describes how quarks behave deep within atomic nuclei. Nothingness is a precarious state of affairs. A state that has no quarks and antiquarks

---

[38] Frank Wilczek, *A Beautiful Question: Finding Nature's Deep Design* (New York: Penguin, 2015), 277.

[39] Ervin Laszlo, *Quantum Shift in a Global Brain: How the New Science of Reality Can Change Us and Our World* (Rochester, VT: Inner Traditions, 2008), 95.

in it is totally unstable.[40] Apparently, a state of something is a more natural state than nothing.

Frank Close of the University of Oxford points out that, according to quantum theory, there is no state of "emptiness," because emptiness would have zero energy. The uncertain quantum world is a vacuum filled with particles that pop in and out of existence. Close believes that all things in our universe are excitations of the quantum vacuum.[41] But these excitations do not appear to be blindly random in effect.

In his study of how we can explain the origins of the creativity of life, evolutionary biologist Andreas Wagner found that creative adaptations of life are driven not just by chance but by a set of laws that allows nature to discover new molecules and mechanisms in a fraction of the time that random variation would take. He says when we study nature, "we learn that life's creativity draws from a source that is older than life, and perhaps older than time."[42]

From the deepest parts of us, our core, there are eruptions from our unconscious minds or perhaps from the collective unconscious. The intuition, the flash of insight, the *Eureka!* moment comes from a place where we have no control, where there is no thought—the core. Once experienced, we seek to connect the core event with our other levels to discern meaning and applications of that event.

In yoga, the goal is to descend through the levels of waking consciousness to unconscious dreaming, to subconscious deep sleep, and finally to absolute consciousness, the one Reality of nothingness, the core, where love is the primary energy. Teilhard de Chardin wrote: "Someday, after mastering the winds, the waves, the tides and gravity, we shall harness for God the energies of love, and then, for a second time in the history of the world, man will have discovered fire."[43]

---

[40] Wilczek, *A Beautiful Question*, 246–47.

[41] Frank Close, *Nothing: A Very Short Introduction* (Oxford: Oxford University Press, 2009).

[42] Andreas Wagner, *Arrival of the Fittest: How Nature Innovates* (New York: Penguin, 2014), 221.

[43] Pierre Teilhard de Chardin, *Toward the Future* (New York: Mariner Books, 2002).

The fire that Teilhard equates with God's energies of love is a great metaphor for the core. The core is what is deepest in us and in our traditions. It is the source, the oneness at the innermost strands of our being. This is the destination of any pilgrimage to a holy place. It is the sacred drive, a longing for union that the mystics in all religious traditions continue to search for and pray to be remembered by and connected. It is a theology of radical immanence.[44]

Francis Rothluebber describes the divine infinite Love-Energy that called "into being that first bit of matter that already contained the future Universe." That matter "began to radiate and expand into a roiling ocean and continues to expand and develop this sharing of divine Love-Energy [that] is the pulsing Heart of the Universe."[45] This is an interesting concept of the core. In this sense, Love-Energy is our essence.

In the core there is no thought; there is only silence, darkness, mystery, nothingness, the void, the abyss of being without form, ground of being, the cloud of unknowing, sacred nothingness. It is nameless and without image. Yet, because something is more natural than nothing, from this sacred nothingness the archetypes emerge. It is the Generative Reality.

> In the beginning,
> There was neither existence nor nonexistence,
> All this world was unmanifest energy. . . .
> The One breathed, without breath, by Its own
>   power
> Nothing else was there. (Rig-Veda)

The Divine in all religious traditions is described by negatives (what God is not), yet it is experienced as the ground of being. This is Apophatic Divinity, which manifests in creation in the bedrock.

Karen Armstrong says:

---

[44] Newell, *The Rebirthing of God*, 7.

[45] Francis Rothluebber, *Who Creates the Future: Discovering the Essential Energy of Co-Creation* (Lawrenceville, NJ: Womanspace, 2016), 6.

The sages [of India] were convinced that if they could access the innermost core of their being they would achieve
unity with the Brahman, "the All," the indestructible and
imperishable energy that fuels the cosmos, establishes its
laws, and pulls all the disparate parts of the universe together.[46]

Underhill's third form of contemplation of the divine Reality
describes the core. After the journey through the first and second
levels of contemplation, she says:

The journey has been a long one; and the hardships and
obstacles involved in it, the effort, the perpetual conscious
pressing forward [have ceased]. Now . . . you feel curiously
lost. . . . No need to push on any further: yet, though there
is no more that you can do of yourself, there is much that
may and must be done to you. . . .

[Now you should] be wisely passive; in order that the
great influences which surround you may take and adjust
your spirit. . . . Let yourself go; cease all conscious, anxious
striving and pushing.

And as you do thus, there will come to you an ever
clearer certitude that this darkness unveils the goal for
which you have been seeking from the first; the final Reality with which you are destined to unite, the perfect satisfaction of your most ardent and most sacred desires. It is
there, but you cannot by your efforts reach it. . . .

You must, so far as you are able, give yourself up to,
"die into," melt into the Whole; abandon all efforts to lay
hold of It. More, you must be willing that it should lay
hold of you. . . .

Here all one can say is this: that if you acquiesce in the
heroic demands which the spiritual life now makes upon
you, if you let yourself go, eradicate the last traces of self-
interest even of the most spiritual kind—then, you have es-
tablished conditions under which the forces of the spiritual
world can work on you, heightening your susceptibilities,

---

[46] Karen Armstrong, *Twelve Steps to a Compassionate Life* (New
York: Anchor Books, 2010), 33.

deepening and purifying your attention, so that you are able to taste and feel more and more of the inexhaustible riches of Reality. . . .

Those ineffective, half-conscious attempts towards free action, clear apprehension, true union, which we dignify by the names of will, thought, and love are now seen matched by an Absolute Will, Thought, and Love; instantly recognized by the contemplating spirit as the highest reality it yet has known, and evoking in it a passionate and a humble joy.[47]

Interaction of the Three Dimensions at the Core

At the core there is no distinction between body, mind, and soul. There is no consciousness, no memory, and no cognition. An experience at the core would perhaps be a deep trance, dreamless sleep, or the "cloud of unknowing."

Conclusion

In this discussion of the strata of reality, the emphasis has been on the connectivity of the strata and the integration of the dimensions of body, mind, and soul within each stratum. In Chapter 3 I describe this connectivity as a cycle and a spiral.

To bring this chapter to a close it is useful to reflect on how each stratum (or "stage," in Underhill's account) leads to the other and why this is important. We descend to the deep bedrock and core and rise to the surface of our lives. Underhill's final words are inspiring:

Each new stage achieved in the mystical development of the spirit has meant, not the leaving behind of the previous stages, but an adding on to them: an ever greater extension of experience, and enrichment of personality. . . .

Thus ascending to the mysterious fruition of that Reality which is beyond image, and descending again to the loving contemplation and service of all struggling growing things,

---

[47] Underhill, *Practical Mysticism*, 72–77.

it now finds and adores everywhere—in the sky and the nest, the soul and the void—one Energetic Love which "is measureless, since it is all that exists." . . .

You correspond, too, with a larger, deeper, broader world. The sky and the hedges, the wide lands through which you are moving, the corporate character and meaning of the group to which you belong—all these are now within the circle of your consciousness; and each little event, each separate demand or invitation which . . . comes to you is now seen in a truer proportion, because you bring to it your awareness of the Whole.

Therefore contemplation, even at its highest, dearest, and most intimate, is not to be for you an end in itself. It shall only be truly yours when it impels you to action: when the double movement of Transcendent Love, drawing inwards to unity and fruition, and rushing out again to creative acts, is realised in you. You are to be a living, ardent tool with which the Supreme Artist works: one of the instruments of His self-manifestation, the perpetual process by which His Reality is brought into concrete expression.[48]

---

[48] Ibid., 81–88.

Chapter 3

Progressing toward Wholeness

Our personality on the surface stratum is the vehicle we live in, but it is not all of who we are. As we progress toward wholeness, we journey inward to experience our emotions and intuitions of a greater reality. We are pulled inward to find deeper meaning and unconditional love.

The wholeness we experience is always in transition. The process of catholicity moves from one state of wholeness, through dissonance, tension and conflict, to greater states of wholeness. This is happening in every aspect of reality we experience as the evolving world.

At any given time we may experience wholeness, health, and order. At other times we experience life as broken, sick, or chaotic. The change from a whole state to unwholeness and fragmentation and back to a new or renewed whole state happens in healing, learning, transformation, and conflict resolution. Catholicity is this process that is progressing toward wholeness.

Resisting this process is counterproductive. When we accept the process a new creative wholeness of life will emerge.[1]

The wholeness model provides a way to understand and apply the progressive processes of becoming whole. The analogy of a spring may be helpful. Springs arise deep within the earth. Because the water is filtered through rocks, it is "both purified and

---

[1] Ilia Delio, *Making All Things New: Catholicity, Cosmology, Consciousness* (Maryknoll, NY: Orbis Books, 2015), 82.

enriched by the minerals that are dissolved."[2] The spring "acts like a fountain, welling up to the surface of its own accord . . . and its waters become available to quench the thirst of humans, animals, and Earth itself."[3]

As an analogy, the three dimensions of the wholeness model we experience on the surface (body, mind, and soul) are nourished by the living water of the bedrock and middle strata that finds its generativity in the core. The flows of energy, wisdom, and love to the surface, like the spring, do so of their own accord, but we also have the capacity to tap into their life-affirming waters.

This chapter explains how we can initiate and experience the flow between the strata and the core. I call this process *cycling* to denote the repeating movement through the strata of the wholeness model in all facets of our lives. Cycling creates a progression that can also be viewed as spiraling into a future of greater complexity.

When we cycle through the strata we bridge the two domains of faith and science. Even for those who consider faith and science as separate, journeying back and forth creates an integration. When I first began to study Christianity, I remember the caution to have the Bible in one hand and the *New York Times* in the other.

In any organism or system the cycling can begin in any strata. Our experiences with the tangible world on the surface move us to the middle, where we have inner sensations, emotions, and images. We then often move to the bedrock to find new possibilities, wisdom and the Love-Energy of God. At the bedrock we find the motivation to move back to the middle with new sensations, feelings, and ideas and then to the surface to put them into action. In cycling, we may even go deep into the core as do the mystical religious traditions and come back to the surface for action as in the Western traditions.

The cycling may begin in the middle where the turbulent liquids, gases, emotions, and thoughts move us to the surface to act

----

[2] Diane Bergant, *A New Heaven, a New Earth: The Bible and Catholicity* (Maryknoll, NY: Orbis Books, 2016), 24.

[3] Ibid., 24–25.

or to the bedrock where we can find intuition and imagination and a sense of connection to the sacred.

In the bedrock things just are, not right or wrong, only possibilities constantly in motion. The coherence of quantum particles described by the quantum biologist is a good metaphor for the coherence that is inherent in the bedrock. The field of emotional physiology has discovered that there are beneficial changes in the nervous, immune, and hormonal systems when we experience emotion such as appreciation, care, compassion, and love. Practical techniques and technologies have been developed that increase sustained physiological coherence.

The coherence of wisdom and love is the "living water" that flows up through the middle and into our life on the surface. It is not until cycling brings these nutrients to the surface and creates coherence that we ascribe meaning and value. As concepts and tangible objects emerge at the surface, we name them, circumscribe them, and judge them.

Figure 3–1 shows that there are three cycles in the model. The first is a cycle between the surface and the middle. What is happening at the surface triggers activity in the middle. These could

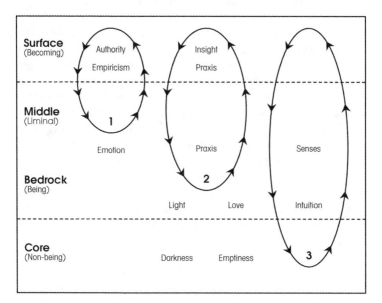

Figure 3–1. Three Cycles of Becoming

be negative impacts, such as gastric upset or negative emotions. Or they could be a positive, such as feelings of joy. Conversely, what is happening in the middle affects our life on the surface, either positively or negatively.

The second cycle is between the surface and the bedrock. This will always have a positive outcome because the state in the bedrock, by definition, serves the best interest of the self on the surface, even if at first it is startling or scary, such as a nightmare.

The third cycle is between the surface and the core. This may be a frequent cycle for those who are spiritually aware, but it is a cycle less taken by those stuck in following the ego on the surface.

In any case, our body, mind, and soul dimensions are continually self-organizing as we cycle through the strata of reality. Delio describes this process poetically: "Nature is like a choreographed ballet or a symphony, whereby an organism is dynamically engaged in its own self-organization, pursuing its own ends amid an ever-shifting context of relationships."[4]

Avoiding "Stuckness" and Making Progress

Our body (physical self), our mind (including personality) and our soul (our deep spiritual dimension) develop as we cycle through the strata. Cycling enables us to tune into the changes that are happening to ourselves, to close friends, our neighbors, our nation, and indeed the whole world. The energy and intelligence that are inherent in the universe are animating our body, mind, and soul at this very moment. If we don't continually cycle, our worldviews and interpretations of events inevitably become fossilized and do not adapt to current realities.

Without cycling, we become stuck in viewing life through only one lens. By cycling through new theories, data, experiences, insights, and ideas, new potentials continually emerge. We create conditions within ourselves for something to emerge that has never existed before.

---

[4] Ilia Delio, *The Unbearable Wholeness of Being: God, Evolution and the Power of Love* (Maryknoll, NY: Orbis Books, 2013), 32.

Each cycle uniquely affects the patterns of our lives. When we gain something from a cycle, we progress in our general well-being. We become more than we were.

As we cycle through the strata of the dimensions of body, mind, and soul, we are renewed and reenergized for what is needed at the surface. I believe that Spirit animates the cycling process and raises our awareness and consciousness of the possibilities in each stratum. Over time, as the content in each stratum changes and becomes more complex, our cycling is enriched.

To illustrate how the cycling works, see Figure 3–2.

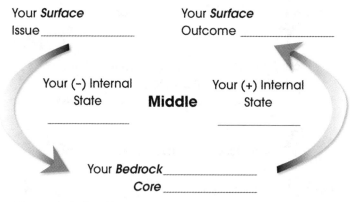

Figure 3–2. Cycles of Becoming

To put the cycle in motion, let's say you have an issue on the surface of acute loss. You are unsure what to do next. After that first step of identifying the issue, you move to the middle to see what is happening internally with your nervous system and your emotions of grief or anger (or both). Use mindful meditation or prayer to create an open, receptive, nonjudgmental awareness of your present moment of stress.[5]

---

[5] Mindfulness meditation creates more communication among the portions of the brain that process stress, brings about focus and calm, and lowers levels of a marker of unhealthy inflammation in the blood. If the molecules are quickened in our endocrine and nervous systems, we naturally experience enhanced blood flow, oxygen supply and consumption, and metabolism (Gretchen Reynolds, "How Meditation Changes the Brain and the Body," *New York Times* February 18, 2016, 20).

With continued reflection you move to the bedrock to see new possibilities and awareness of the Love-Energy that is available to you. When you are ready, you return to the middle and note any changes in your mood and your body.

It is to be hoped that there is a positive improvement that motivates you to act on the surface. The result should be a happier outlook, better understanding and acceptance of reality, and more compassion for the world around you, including yourself (see Figure 3–3).

Your **Surface**
Issue: *Acute loss*

Your **Surface**
Outcome: *Compassion*

Your (–) Internal
State
Grief/anger

Middle

Your (+) Internal
State
Forgiveness

Your **Bedrock**   Love-energy
Core   Apophatic Divinity

Figure 3–3. Overcoming a Sense of Loss

The cycling process is similar to the Lectio Divina, which describes a way of reading the scriptures whereby a person gradually lets go of his or her own agenda and opens to inspiration by the Divine.

First, a short passage of scripture is slowly read and absorbed. The second stage is reflection on the text to take from it what God wants to give. The third stage is to leave thinking aside and let the heart speak to God. The final stage is to let go of one's own thoughts and to listen at a deep level to God who speaks within. As we listen, we are gradually transformed.

My favorite metaphor about cycling, perhaps because I am half Finnish, is the story of the hero Väinämöinen in the Finnish epic of Kalevala. He wounded his leg with an axe while cutting a tree. He could heal his leg only by cycling down to find the origins of the axe blade and the handle. By understanding the origin of the causes of his afflictions, he could find healing. The cycle of becoming similarly helps us to understand what is beneath and what causes the current situation at the surface.

Linking Conscious and Unconscious

In Jungian psychology the bedrock would be considered the domain of our personal unconscious and the collective unconscious. The energy in the unconscious has a timeless and spaceless quality. It is unpredictable and may burst forth in our emotions in the middle and our conscious mind on the surface at any time—certainly in dreams occurring as we awaken, but also in moments of crisis, moments of relaxation (for example, while in the shower), or when we actively try to engage the unconscious (see Chapter 5).

In Jungian therapy the goal is to cycle to the unconscious by analyzing dreams to bring the unconscious contents into the conscious mind and into a relationship with the conscious ego. Cycling brings about the emergence of the Self as our center that can integrate the conscious and the unconscious. To become fully human we must connect to what is unconscious and the waves of probability at the bedrock and bring it to awareness at the surface.

The cycling in waking moments is like going to sleep through the stages of sleeping from light sleep to deep sleep where most dreams occur and reaching the collective unconscious described by Jung.

For many in science "the issue of inner mental experience" is critical.[6] What is the mind? What is consciousness? Marcelo Gleiser refers to an "island of knowledge on a sea of mystery."[7] In the mysterious interplay of matter and spirit (body and soul), mind is a subjective dimension of reality that pervades the universe.

Roger Penrose and Stuart Hameroff argue that our biology evolved and adapted to access the quantum realm and to maximize the qualities and potentials implicit within it. The coherent

---

[6] Sean Carroll, *The Big Picture: On the Origins of Life, Meaning, and the Universe Itself* (New York: Dutton, 2016).

[7] Marcelo Gleiser, *The Island of Knowledge: The Limits of Science and the Search for Meaning* (New York: Basic Books, 2014).

quantum activity among the microtubules in our brain allows us to amplify or strengthen the basic universal consciousness that is already there. When we meditate and attain nothingness, it isn't quite nothingness. We move more deeply into the quantum realm, the basic fabric of the universe, and the world of wisdom and light that is the foundation of all things, and we become more consciously a part of it.[8]

Most of our living goes on without our being conscious of it. All the activity of the atoms, the molecules, the cells in our bodies, and many of our physical processes of the body function without our awareness. We emerge into consciousness from the unconscious every morning as we awake.

Cycling reconciles or balances our conscious awareness with information that we have repressed or that comes from the collective wisdom in the universe.

By cycling we become more deeply aware about what is unknown, unconscious, or hidden in the psyche. By holding a creative tension between what is happening on the surface and the unknown and unpredictable possibilities in the bedrock, something new can emerge. Holding the tension opens us up to the mediating influences of a transcendent force and the emergence of a transformation. Jung called this mediating force the transcendent function, which is the space or field that mediates between the conscious and unconscious.[9]

The line we create between surface material reality, our middle emotions, and our deep capacity of connection at the bedrock is not a line at all. The essence of reality is a self-creating flow of energy and information.

Our consciousness is an open system, constantly changing in new and creative ways, achieving new levels of consciousness as it forms relationships and connections with its environment. The

---

[8] Stuart Hameroff and Roger Penrose, "Consciousness in the Universe: A Review of the 'Orch OR' Theory," *Phys Life Rev* 11, no. 1 (March 2014): 39–78.

[9] Jeffrey C. Miller, *The Transcendent Function: Jung's Model of Psychological Growth through Dialogue with the Unconscious* (Albany: SUNY Press, 2004); Edwin E. Olson, "The Transcendent Function in Organization Change," *Journal of Applied Behavioral Science* 26, no. 1 (1990): 69–81.

creative process entails going to the bedrock where, although ambiguous and uncomfortable, generative creativity happens.

Cycling to the Middle Stratum

Emotions in the middle are just below the surface of our personalities. They drive our behavior. Conflict on the surface inflames, distorts, and degrades the ego; it creates a turmoil of emotions in the middle. When there is harmony on the surface, cycling to the middle triggers positive feelings that support the cooperative behavior on the surface.

In 1985, in his critiques of public communications in America, including the content and biases of the news media, Neil Postman said we have a "loop of impotence."[10] He says: "The news elicits from you a variety of opinions about which you can do nothing except to offer them as more news, about which you can do nothing.[11] This is being stuck in a cycle between the surface and the middle. We go back and forth seeing what is happening, then feeling bad or angry about it, and then returning to our observations. If we fear the intensity of our fears and anger in the middle, we devise strategies to control or deny these emotions. We can become used to this loop of impotence and adapt it as part of our identity. To get out of the loop of impotence that Postman describes, we need to cycle deep to the bedrock or core to gain inspiration and wisdom and come back for action at the surface.

Cycling to the Bedrock

Cycling to the bedrock is going to a deep level where there is a dynamic, living potential that is always active. Muhammad asked his followers to make an existential "surrender" (*islam*) of their entire being to Allah. "A *muslim* was a man or woman who had made this surrender of ego," for example, by prostrating himself

---

[10] Neil Postman, *Amusing Ourselves to Death: Public Discourse in the Age of Show Business* (New York: Penguin, 1985).

[11] Ibid., 69.

or herself "in prayer several times a day" to learn that surrendering to a level deeper than the rational mind "entailed daily transcendence of the preening, prancing ego."[12]

In Zen Buddhism "the spiritual journey is a ceaseless process of investigating ourselves, of digging through the layers of our conditioning to reach the ground of our being."[13]

In the various mystic traditions there are several pathways to the altered state of consciousness encountered in the spiritual bedrock. One path uses deep concentration and contemplation to reach a drowsy state and meditation practices such as yoga to reach a deep trance. Another path is to use stimulation, including chanting and dance, to reach a state of ecstasy.

Cycling to the bedrock requires us to trust the wholeness that is living in us by "dancing" with the turbulence, the obstacles in the middle strata, so that our coherent self at the bedrock connects to our active self at the surface.

We give up the illusion of control and enter a condition of profound trust that something larger than us loves us. The goal of the cycle is learning to relax, letting go of a sense of vigilance, surrendering moment by moment, reveling in the now, and recognizing a compelling dynamic.

For those who are uncomfortable with God language, the cycle to the bedrock can be viewed as going to an inner aliveness, meaning, and sacredness in the universe that nourishes a sense of integration and communion. Brian McLaren calls this spiritual journey "seeking vital connection."[14]

If we stay connected to the coherence in the bedrock, our deep inner connection will flow up to the middle, and through prayer and meditation, on up to our life on the surface. The spiritual bedrock can provide an eruption of awe into everyday lives in startling, breathtaking moments and an orientation of wholeness to living.

---

[12] Karen Armstrong, *Twelve Steps to a Compassionate Life* (New York: Anchor Books, 2010), 60.

[13] John Daido Loori, *Riding the Ox Home: Stages on the Path of Enlightenment* (Boston: Shambhala, 2002), x.

[14] Brian D. McLaren, *Naked Spirituality: A Life with God in Twelve Simple Words* (New York: HarperOne, 2012).

What makes the elemental human experience of awe significant is it is, first and foremost, an experience of meaning. It saturates the world with meaning. Explanations for the origins of that meaning must always come later.[15]

If our ego breaks that connection, we experience fear, stress, and even physical distress. By staying connected to the bedrock we live with the sense that a divine presence is operating in and through us. Carl Rogers calls this "unconditional positive regard."[16]

The bedrock for religious people is like a deep well gushing forth living waters. Living in connection to the bedrock and going into the deep living waters is to be overwhelmed by the light and love of God.

John Philip Newell suggests praying to find the courage to cycle deep to the bedrock to be whole and to find strength to act at the surface:

Pray to God that we have the courage to feel, together to weep, and the deepest in us to flow into holy courage to act. Then when we cry for help, God will say "Here I am." This One is the seeing, weeping center for healing. Our true strength is here, now, deep in us.[17]

Cycling to the Core

In the description of the strata in Chapter 2, Underhill provided an account of how mystics experience God in each stratum. As we cycle over time, it is likely that our conception and image of God will change. Even lofty, mystical words used to image God, such as the *ground of being, the holy, the divine presence,* even *quantum sea of light,* will seem inadequate.

---

[15] Adam Frank, "Is Atheist Awe a Religious Experience?" 13.7 Cosmos and Culture blog, NPR, September 16, 2014.

[16] Carl Rogers, *A Way of Being* (New York: Mariner Books, 1995).

[17] John Philip Newell, Sermon at Chautauqua, New York, The Chautauqua Institution, August 5, 2016.

The divine presence in us is the magnetism that creates bedrock coherence, analogous to the powerful magnets in an MRI machine that put the hydrogen atoms in our body into alignment—just as the atoms in the brains of a European robin are affected by the earth's magnetic field.

This magnetism is not a controlling force, but it has a profound effect on our lives. The presence has the soft qualities of love, vulnerability, and forgiveness. Those forces are inherently indeterminate in the sense that they cannot force any particular outcome. When we surrender to this magnetic presence, we trust that it is acting in our best interests. Jesus surrendered to this presence by conquering the Roman Empire with Love-Energy, not force and violence.

It is provocative to think that this divine magnetism that creates coherence in the bedrock may come from the core. As we hope and pray for coherence, perhaps we receive it from that deep unknowing, the Apophatic Divinity we cannot comprehend, or, as the apostle Paul describes it, "the peace that passes understanding" (Phil 4:7). We long for a connection to God that transforms us. Bruce Sanguin contrasts desire and longing this way:

One of the core competencies of evolutionary spirituality is the capacity to distinguish between desire and longing. It is a subtle distinction, because neither will ever be fulfilled. Desire is typically for more of what we already have. It is craving. Longing, on the other hand, is for a deepening. "From the depths I cry to you, O G_d." Desire creates habits, neurological and behavioral loops that keep us locked into yesterday. Longing opens us up to new neural pathways being laid down, and breaks us out of routine, making room for a new and more intense future. Desire issues in routines and ruts. In the temporary satisfaction of desire, we may feel free, but it lands us back where we started. Longing leads to adventure and to authentic freedom. It requires risk as an orientation in life. Unfulfilled desire leads to increased contraction, anxiety, and isolation. Unfulfilled longing is expansive. In fact, true longing is not meant to be satiated. It causes us to wonder where we are being led. It connects us more deeply to life, to love, and to freedom.[18]

Cycling to the core is to give up ego and surrender to the will of divine presence that will contribute to a meaningful life on the surface. Space and time cease to matter as we embrace the mystery of now. Dissonance, conflicts, contradictions are washed away. My personal experience of cycling in the core is not the presence of a "personal" God, but rather a sense of overflowing, and overwhelming deep mystery. My response is gratitude, silence, tears, joy, and surrender to the infinite I am experiencing. Another's personal experience may have a very different sense to it yet be just as much in touch with the core.

Delio's statement about the cycling that occurs in evolution is suggestive of what it is like to cycle to the core:

> [Cycling] is not repetition of the old world or a cyclic return to the beginning but an ever newness of life born out of the ever newness of love. Divine love is not a river of stagnant water but a fountain fullness of overflowing love, love that is forever awakening to new life. God is ever newness in love and the power of everything new in love.[19]

The cycling to the core is an evolution toward inner wholeness and wisdom, knowing oneself as a participant in divine energy. Newell says:

> The wisdom of God is deep within us. Within us as a sheer gift of God is the capacity to bring forth what has never been seen before, including what has never been imaged before. Deep within us are holy, natural longings for oneness, primal sacred drives for union. The *Rebirthing of God* is pointing to a radical reemergence of the Divine from deep

---

[18] Bruce Sanguin, *The Way of the Wind: The Path and Practice of Evolutionary Christian Mysticism* (Vancouver: Viriditas Press, 2015), 45.

[19] Delio, *The Unbearable Wholeness of Being*, 77.

within us. We do not have to create it. We cannot create it. But we can let it spring forth and be reborn in our lives.[20]

When we reach the divine presence in the core, we feel at ease and experience a sense of quiet peace. Our soul is touched as we experience the mystery of the whole.

Matthew Fox quotes Meister Eckhart when observing that we journey deep into the very ground of hearing to hear the divine Word, which "lies hidden in the soul in such a way that one does not know it or hear it. Unless room is made in the ground of hearing, it cannot be heard; indeed, all voices and sound must go out, and there must be absolute silence there and stillness."[21] This describes our need to go to the core for absolute silence and stillness.

Cycling to the Kingdom of God

The teaching and practices of Jesus provide excellent examples of cycling to the divine presence. Jesus wanted his followers to live by accessing their spontaneous inner wisdom, often referred to as the kingdom of God within. By so doing, the disciples could tap into and experience the joy and love of the presence of God. Bruce Sanguin describes it this way:

> Jesus channeled a creative power that was wild, unpredictable, and iconoclastic . . . a freedom which flows from an interior condition wherein one is liberated, moment by moment, to respond intuitively to the promptings of Spirit.[22]

Jesus's message was that to be awakened and liberated from consensus reality we need to see everything on the surface, no

[20] John Philip Newell, *The Rebirthing of God: Christianity's Struggle for New Beginnings* (Woodstock, VT: Skylight Paths Publishing, 2015), x.

[21] Matthew Fox, *Meister Eckhart: A Mystic Warrior for Our Times* (Novato, CA: New World Library, 2014), 3.

[22] Sanguin, *The Way of the Wind*, 71–72.

matter how mundane, as an opening to the Divine at the bedrock and core.

Bruce Sanguin explains what Jesus meant by entering the kingdom of God:

> To enter the kingdom of God, Jesus's apostles were required to have some capacity for an interior life, for conscious self-awareness, to be or to become a mystic. This is a shift from seeing through a lens of fragmentation and alienation to seeing the wholeness that is animating and living all of life. Even in this midst of suffering, disease, and oppression, this Wholeness . . . is waiting to be realized—symbolized in the gospels by the prevalence of healing stories.[23]

The kingdom of God is within the hidden depths of the bedrock. When made conscious, the kingdom manifests in the outer world. Our life at the surface is animated by the bedrock energy of the spirit. When the connection to the bedrock is cut off, ignored, or rejected, our life on the surface can be idolatrous.

To illustrate that we can rise above our self-imposed limitations, limitations imposed by others, and our unconscious assumptions and beliefs, we can look at Jesus's conversation with Nicodemus. Jesus asked Nicodemus to die to his former self and former life and be born as a new creation—letting go of everything that everybody else thought was important.

For Nicodemus, it meant letting go his attachment to his status, theological acumen, and the carefully constructed beliefs for which he was known and honored. Nicodemus came to Jesus because he was uncertain and anxious about his life. Jesus urged him to go to the bedrock, where he could let go of his egoic self and trust in the Spirit to be created as a different person, one who is divine.

Apparently, this was a stretch too far for Nicodemus, at least that night. However, he later risks his reputation by openly assisting in the burial of Jesus (John 19:39–42), so perhaps he was able further to consider Jesus's words at a later time and continue in the cycle.

---

[23] Bruce Sanguin, "The Kin(g)dom of G_d, Idolatry, and Healing," blog.

Conclusion

The cycle of becoming provides a way to understand continuous change and how we can affect it. We often make assumptions about the permanence of things, and unbeknown to us, small changes over time at the micro level in the bedrock are producing big changes, sometimes quickly. We also assume we are in control of things, but then find things are happening beyond our control.

To attain greater wholeness, we cannot be stuck at one level or in one dimension. We must keep cycling, going through all the levels in all three dimensions. We need to live dialectically in all three strata at once, being grounded in time and space at the surface but also grounded in the bedrock of possibilities and the core of divine knowing.

The differences in each dimension contribute to an overall sense of purpose and progression from simple to complex, from material to existential riches, from aloneness to community.

If the cycle were only a random process with unlimited freedom, outcomes would be totally unpredictable. If the cycle were regulated and controlled, we would be limited to an outcome of conformity. Many possibilities can emerge in any given cycle, but because the primary energy at the bedrock and core is love, all outcomes will effectuate and be ordered by love.

When I experience cycling through the strata, I encounter a series of processes that I view in their totality as my self. I can think of myself as a "selfing" process, a self-organizing continuous creation that I localize in an "Edwin." From early childhood I have been learning and telling a story about me that has grown over time to a strong sense of self. My story has spread it out to others. My self is the effect I have in the world. When I am animated by the core and bedrock, my more mature self expresses this. When I am animated only by my surface identity and my middle emotions, my self is constrained.

My spiritual work is to relax that control and constriction so I can be a clear reflection of the Source that is manifesting as my true self. The constraints are in my culture and history but also in my freedom. Trauma and shadow work is necessary to break through to higher consciousness. I need to focus on the process that cycling suggests and ask what is living in me that wants to come through. The whole biosphere is an evolving process. I need to recognize I am part of that process.

Chapter 4

The Wholeness Narrative

Scientific inquiry has given us a narrative of the epic of evolution—the universe story where humans and human cultures emerged from and, hence, are a part of nature—the body and mind dimensions. Religious believers and spiritual seekers have developed interpretive, spiritual, and moral/ethical responses to that scientific narrative, informed by their belief in the presence of the Divine—the soul dimension. In Chapters 1–3 I used the wholeness and cycle of becoming models to suggest how the three dimensions can be integrated.

I invite the reader to contemplate what has been covered in the preceding three chapters to see if this information can be put into an understandable and useful personal wholeness narrative. Nothing as succinct as $E=mc^2$, but a story that you can tell your friends and colleagues.

To be useful and meaningful, a narrative needs to sync with the other stories people tell themselves. A personal narrative of becoming whole through cycling through the surface, middle, and bedrock strata of the three dimensions of body, mind, and soul needs to be understood in the context of larger and more inclusive stories. One's scientific worldview and religious tradition provide the larger stories within which individual stories make sense and without which they cannot.[1]

---

[1] John A. Teske, "Narrative and Meaning in Science and Religion," *Zygon* 45, no. 1 (March 2010): 100.

Our personal narratives contain the conflicts and tensions we experience, the patterns in our life that capture our attention, and our hopes for the future. The cycle of becoming shows how our reality is continuously being constructed from our interactions in and between the three strata of surface, middle, and bedrock and the three dimensions of body, mind, and soul. Much is happening at all three strata and the three dimensions of reality, but it is hard for us to remember that we are supposed to be awed by it all.

Robert Funk in his 1985 inaugural address to the newly formed Jesus Seminar said:

> What we need is a new fiction . . . a new story that reaches beyond old beginnings and endings. . . . Not any fiction will do. . . . We require a new liberating fiction, one that squares with the best knowledge we can now accumulate and one that transcends self-serving ideologies.[2]

Collectively, we need a story that can restore idealism and overcome a sense of isolation and fragmentation. We need a story that brings us back from selfishness, cynicism, distrust, and autonomy. The new story needs to emphasize love, the dignity of our lives, friendship, faithfulness, solidarity, and neighborliness.

The story needs to be inspiring—giving a sense of awe that there is something larger and more mysterious than our individual lives. We need to be humble and self-confident, surrendering to grace, and powerful. We need to be brave to embrace a new story and express it in some new way that will be compelling for others.

Robert Wright quotes William James that religion "consists of the belief that there is an unseen order, and that our supreme good lies in harmoniously adjusting ourselves thereto."[3] Wright says that science's version of the unseen order is the laws of nature. If the two kinds of order can themselves be put into harmony, in

---

[2] Robert Funk, "Inaugural Address," *Foundations and Facets Forum* 1.1, Jesus Seminar (1985), 14–15.

[3] William James, *The Varieties of Religious Experience* (1902), quoted in Robert Wright, *The Evolution of God* (Boston, MA: Back Bay Books, 2010), 27.

that adjustment may lie a supreme good. The new narrative must be inclusive of both kinds of unseen order. All views must be heard. The new narrative must be capable of learning about other people's truth and how their lives are different. In formulating the new narrative we need to ask if it includes everybody.

The new narrative would be most effective if it could cut through our most common illusions:

Illusion of permanence. Everything is constantly evolving. Changes at the micro level can confound predictions at the macro level. "You can't step into the same river twice" (Heraclitus). A small change of one degree becomes big over time.

Illusion of separation. Every faith points to the absolute Reality beyond our physical state where all difference ceases to exist and where only absolute truth prevails. There is no duality—only unity and enlightenment. In a quantum view of the world we are entangled. Our ego creates the illusion that we are separate.

Illusion of appearance. What we see is not ultimate Reality. For mystics, the material world reflects the absolute existence. Beyond and underneath the material world is dark matter and energy, quantum mechanics, and the relativity of everything pointed to by scientists.

Illusion of control. In mysticism the sense of self submerges into the Divine. When we are submerged in God, God acts through us. The universe, our biosphere, our self, and our relationships are constantly self-organizing. We can influence the patterns that emerge in these self-organizing processes, but we can't predict or control the outcomes.[4]

Delio says that the impasse we are in, "the inability of ecclesial and cultural systems [and I would add political systems[to cooperate for the welfare of humankind," results from "the lack of a fundamental meta-narrative." There is no "overarching story that unites us and instills hope and courage. . . . We need a larger story that can include diversity and difference, and in which our local stories can thrive."[5]

---

[4] Edwin E. Olson and Glenda H. Eoyang, *Facilitating Organization Change: Lessons from Complexity Science* (San Francisco, CA: Jossey-Bass/Pfeiffer, 2001).

[5] Ilia Delio, *The Unbearable Wholeness of Being: God, Evolution, and the Power of Love* (Maryknoll, NY: Orbis Books, 2013), xiv, xv.

A Mystical Narrative

The narrative that I have presented about the wholeness of body, mind, and soul is not literal. The mind and soul dimensions are metaphors, modeled after the body dimension, which is grounded in the science of quantum biology. The narrative could be considered as myth, that is, as the deeper meaning of the life we experience. I am guided by this myth, although I cannot verify how it happens. I have bolstered the myth by bringing together (1) our current understanding of empirical reality as revealed by science; (2) the intuitions about reality from consciousness studies; and (3) the wisdom of the world's religions, especially the Christian religion, with which I am most familiar.

To apply the wholeness model to one's life it is helpful to be a mystic. At the mystical level everything is whole now, all at once, a unitive, intuitive kind of knowledge and discernment about being and the wholeness of creation.

For Richard Rohr, *mysticism* simply means experiential knowledge of spiritual things, as opposed to book knowledge, secondhand knowledge, seminary or church knowledge. He says that a mystic is a person who has moved from mere belief systems or belonging systems to actual inner experience. He believes that until individuals have had some level of *inner religious experience,* there is no point in asking them to follow religious doctrines. "Moral mandates and doctrinal affirmations only become the source of deeper anxiety and more contentiousness, leading to denial, pretension, and projection of our evil elsewhere."[6]

Jean Houston says myth is an imprint in the psyche and spiritual DNA—"something that never was but is always happening."[7] She quotes Joseph Campbell as saying that "myth is the secret opening through which the inexhaustible energies of the cosmos pour into human cultural manifestation."[8] Myth engages the depth of the psyche.

---

[6] Richard Rohr, "Mystical Experience," blog, January 24–25, 2017.

[7] Jean Houston, *The Search for the Beloved: Jungian Sacred Psychology* (Los Angeles: Jeremy P. Turcher, 1987), 101.

[8] Joseph Campbell, *The Hero with a Thousand Faces,* Bollinger Series XVII (Princeton, NJ: Princeton University Press, 1973), 3.

Houston says that when mythological symbols are not relevant to our lives, "we experience a sense of alienation from society, often followed by a desperate quest to replace the lost meaning of the once powerful myths."[9] Houston believes that the recent decades of exploration of myth in the world's religions is an indication that the stories could be linked together to develop a planetary mythos.[10]

Houston says that the mythic emerges "as spontaneous creations, full and richly detailed realities glimpsed in dreams, in vision, in moments when the walls between the worlds are let down."[11] This has been my experience in writing this book. From an early intuition that the quantum biologists had unlocked a portal to understand the depth of life, to my dreams about that connection, to my study of science, religion, and spirituality, to the unfolding of the theory and its application in leading adult spiritual enrichment groups, to my conversation with Ilia Delio about how it was an expression of catholicity in an evolving universe, and to this book, my journey to the new story is one in which the emerging story and I became one. Houston predicts this will happen for those who follow the sacred process toward wholeness.

Carter Phipps, in his discussion of evolutionary spirituality, emphasizes the importance of touching divinity "not only in the mystical intuitions of a transcendent realm of being but in our own efforts to *become*, to give birth to something more good, true and beautiful in the very processes of the universe's becoming—and ultimately of our own."[12]

The narrative of cycling is about searching and finding something larger that is loving us and of which we can be a part. The dynamic process at the bedrock and core are the evolutionary processes of the earth and the universe. Our responsibility with regard to the evolutionary process is to cooperate, to give up the illusion of control and a sense of vigilance, and to enter a condition of profound trust that the processes are *for* us. They

---

[9] Ibid., 103.

[10] Ibid.

[11] Ibid.

[12] Carter E. Phipps, *Evolutionaries: Unlocking the Spiritual and Cultural Potential of Science's Greatest Idea* (New York: Harper, 2012), 383.

are loving and benevolent. It isn't all up to us. If we surrender moment by moment, we revel in the now.

The cycling force within us enables us to move to the deeper levels of our being so we can develop, evolve, and embrace the far greater realms of what is possible, the "more." This is a sacred impulse, the soul's yearning, a desire for creative emergence, love, adventure, the "zest for life."[13]

Using the Wholeness Model to Be Resilient

The cycle of becoming model points to the continual uncertainty of our life on the surface, the turmoil at the middle stratum, and the hopeful possibilities of what will emerge from the bedrock. While somewhat disquieting, if we approach life knowing that all things contain a measure of uncertainty, we can be more flexible, resilient, and adaptable in improving our lives.

Every living thing and every social system benefits from the unpredictability, randomness, accidents, and chaos that cause systems to self-correct, self-organize, and generate unexpected innovation.[14] A resilient and agile life must be based on an equal amount of certainty and the ability to embrace the complexity, subtlety, and nuances that come with inevitable uncertainty in all three strata and all three dimensions.

In each stratum there are moment-by-moment interactions between differences in the three dimensions. This generates more complexity as new entities emerge, each emergence starting a new interaction that creates another more complex pattern. As each moment dissolves, giving way to the next, there is a flow, a continuity created by the iteration of the interactions. The new entities may remain as a community of numerous subjects or they may synchronize and combine to become a new complex entity, already able to interact with the perpetual change in its internal and external environments.[15]

The core is creative Love-Energy, what is often named as Spirit, pulsating and interacting in all three strata, restlessly

---

[13] Pierre Teilhard de Chardin, *The Divine Milieu* (New York: Harper Perennial Modern Classics, 2001).

[14] Bruce Sanguin, "Evolutionary Christianity," blog.

[15] Emma Restall Orr, *The Wakeful World: Animism, Mind, and the Self in Nature* (Winchester, UK: Moon Books, 2012), 269.

throughout time and eternity. The bedrock is the wellspring of all possibility. The middle contains the energy, emotions, and meditations that flow to the surface and to the bedrock. On the surface all creatures engage co-creatively in the expanding horizon of life. Ultimate meaning and our moral guidelines on the surface are created by cycling through the strata and being transformed with a new and creative understanding of reality.

We only get absolute certainty by stopping the cycling process and pretending that the situation we are facing on the surface is not subject to change.

When we cycle through the wholeness model we have a sense that there is progress in the increasing complexification of life and that there is an infinite destiny in an infinite universe. The progressive spiral of wholeness suggests that death and extinction are an essential part of cosmic evolution.

The mystery that the wholeness model points to is not a problem to be solved or an unknown that will be discovered. The mystery is just "Being," an infinite, shared consciousness in all three dimensions of body, mind, and soul. The cycle of becoming model helps us to participate in the mystery, not to solve it.

The Value of Cycling through the Strata

If we imagine humanity as a living tree, we could say that the bedrock is our largely invisible root system. If we lose or destroy our invisible connection to the sacred bedrock, our wider circles of identity begin to be eroded and undermined and our human ties and communal bonds begin to weaken.

The quantum laws at the bedrock are predictable and give us a robust life in the body dimension. The familiar statistical laws and Newtonian laws are, ultimately, quantum laws that have been filtered through a decoherence lens that screens out the quantum coherence. When things get "big" and "slow," quantum phenomena wash out.

By analogy, we should expect that we can also count on the bedrock of the mind and soul dimensions, because the potential for a higher consciousness and a more mature spirituality is already present at the bedrock. However, we must be attentive to many small insights over many interactions. By cycling through the strata in each dimension, we increase the rate of interactions. We create a fuller reality. The reality we experience as spiritual is the total of the interactions where we experience something more. Physical and mental perceptions are augmented by spiritual insights that often awe and animate us. We may not clearly understand these interactions, but they are fundamental to our being and becoming.

We recognize that these moments are sacred and express them mentally and physically. The accumulation of these experiences constitutes our soul, the wholeness of our self. Jesus confronted all persons he met with a vision of the highest possibility available to them, a future in which their humanity was deepened, liberated, and more aligned with their essential divine nature.

One day Jesus was confronted with the question of fasting. The disciples of John the Baptist and the Pharisees fasted, but Jesus's disciples did not. When asked why, Jesus made several mysterious responses, among them, "No one puts new wine into old wineskins: otherwise, the wine will burst the skins, and the wine is lost, and so are the skins: but one puts new wine into fresh wineskins" (Mark 2:22).

A new wineskin is pliable and can expand as the wine ferments and expands. An old wineskin is not pliable but is rather brittle. The new wineskin of higher possibilities offered by Jesus provides a way to hear and heed the new wisdom, the new wine, arising from interactions with the bedrock.

Jesus activated a depth dimension hidden beneath the individual's surface personality. He lured the person to the bedrock and to a new way of seeing, a new worldview, and a new way of becoming whole and healed.

Living superficially by adhering to external rules and codes of conduct at the surface needs to give way to participating in, and being captured by, a hidden depth dimension at the bedrock, which is the Source of life itself. "Most listeners and readers, then and now, try to understand Jesus' teachings with the mind of the old human, operating from conventional wisdom and morality. . . . [To] understand Jesus we need to undergo a *metanoia*, which means literally receiving a changed mind."[16]

By cycling through the strata, we awaken to the creative impulse in the universe that is manifesting itself in us, through us, and as us. The narrative of the cycle asks us to see things as they

---

[16] Bruce Sanguin, *The Way of the Wind: The Path and Practice of Evolutionary Christian Mysticism* (Vancouver: Viriditas Press, 2015), 56.

are, that they are connected, that they can be changed, and that they are headed somewhere.

Trusting that this process is an extrapersonal, active force affecting us gives even greater urgency to our need to take up our responsibility as co-creators who can take reality as it is and yet seek to transform it so the higher possibilities become more and more probable. The same power out of which galaxies emerged continues to work, in all circumstances, good or bad, in our lives. Once we accept this reality, then we can engage our creative capacities and our personal will to act decisively to enact the future our hearts know is possible.

In summary, I believe that cycling through the model provides a framework for explaining and experiencing how our reality is created, one informed both by science and the practice of spiritual traditions. The cycling demonstrates that

- our lives have a depth beyond our surface personal preferences and desires;
- there is a drive in creation that is urging us to go to the bedrock to find greater intelligence and greater love;
- we can be transformed if we commit to regularly cycle through the strata of reality;
- adopting diet, physical, mental, and spiritual practices at the surface and middle levels facilitates a state of openness to what emerges from the bedrock;
- our journey to the bedrock and back to the surface is being resourced and guided by the Spirit;
- we need to confront the turbulence (emotion) in the middle stratum that gets in the way of our journey to the bedrock;
- we can find specific indicators of how the Spirit is helping on the journey;
- we can make it our mission to creatively live out the new life that emerges from the transformation;
- as we surrender to the Apophatic Divinity at the bedrock and the core, we will find our identity, who we are meant to be; and
- we are not alone in cycling through the strata of reality— we are joining the whole cosmos in the "dance."[17]

---

[17] These ten aspects were inspired by Bruce Sanguin, "Reclaiming Religious Narrative," blog.

Applying the Model in Everyday Life

The new narrative is that reality is one—manifested physically, mentally, and spiritually. The cycle of becoming model shows how this one Reality is constantly changing. New creative patterns emerge with energy and potential for creating new forms and structures. In describing the practice of learning and reverence of an animist, Emma Orr describes the cycling process poetically:

Aspiring to play an active and respectful part in the creative process of life, even if only through gratitude, awe and devotion, [the animist will also recognize] that in the mental and physical form he perceives there is memory and perseverance, there is wisdom, pain and freedom, there are stories of moments flowing into moments, stretching out to the horizons of space and time. . . . The song is the expression of the moment as it unfolds, our soul riding the current of the spirits whose perpetual motion is our becoming. The songs of being are the music of presence. The song is what we express and celebrate in every moment of our living.[18]

In Part II I explain how this narrative can be applied in self-development, relationships, ecology, and moral leadership using specific examples of cycling through the three strata of body, mind, and soul. Readers can apply their own version of this narrative to the challenges and the opportunities in their own lives.

Personally, when I cycle through the strata I am confronted by questions: What is it that I really want? What am I really longing for? It is easy to confuse desire and longing. Bruce Sanguin says:

Desire is typically for more of what we already have. . . . Desire creates habits, neurological and behavioral loops that keep us locked into yesterday. Desire issues in routine

---

[18] Orr, *The Wakeful World*, 270.

and ruts. In the temporary satisfaction of desire, we may feel free, but it lands us back where we started.[19]

Longing, by contrast, is for our larger self that longs for more love, more life, and more ability to see the beauty in everyday life. Using religious language, I believe it is the Spirit that leads me to paradoxically rest in longing.

To connect to my deep longings, I need to take risks, be creative, and expand beyond my constricted self, which keeps me stuck in the old patterns. My constricted, ego-driven self is my wasteful self that contributes to our consumer economy. With a larger self I have the freedom and the option of consciously creating the conditions for transformation for myself, for my friends and family, and for the communities of which I am a part.

I have also found the cycle can be useful to clarify tragedies, accidents, and evils in our society by asking: How and when in the cycling did things happen to create the conditions that led to the effect? What was it that let the tragedy, accident, and evil emerge on the surface?

I can also identify the life-giving patterns I observe and extrapolate and project these patterns into the future. Despite the news headlines of, for example, the mass shooting at a gay bar in Orlando, Florida, in June 2016, the outpouring of love and support for the LGBT community throughout the world was a demonstration of a wholeness, increased empathy, and caring.

My daily goal is to organize my life according to my deep longing. This has slowly begun to shatter the false idols I have confused with life itself.

To begin a cycle, I look for the awe and wonder around me, being open to the complexity that will be revealed. I see the interconnectedness of things and find things I had not known as I see the past and the future in the present moment. I awaken to deep questions for reflection and my potential to transcend conventional wisdom.

---

[19] Sanguin, *The Way of the Wind*, 45.

These questions arise when I use the cycle to reflect on my own life:

- How do my experiences of awe stir me in the bedrock?
- What happens in my environment that creates an inner coherence for me?
- How do I contribute to that coherence?
- How can I increase the length of time I am in a coherent state?
- How can I demonstrate coherence for others?

Eckhart Tolle writes:

The new consciousness is: acceptance, enjoyment, and enthusiasm—each is a certain vibrational frequency of consciousness. You need to be vigilant to make sure that one of them operates whenever you are engaged in doing anything at all—from the simplest task to the most complex. If you are not in the state of either acceptance, enjoyment, or enthusiasm, look closely and you will find that you are creating suffering for yourself and others.[20]

I have found that Tolle's three "vibrational frequencies of consciousness"—acceptance, enjoyment, and enthusiasm—correlate nicely with a positive experience of cycling through the three strata of bedrock (acceptance), middle (enjoyment), and surface (enthusiasm).

If I embrace change and focus on wholeness, I can participate in what Jan Phillips calls an evolutionary leap unlike anything in our history:

There is evidence in the human family of an upward shift in consciousness, a maturing spirituality and a connectedness that grows more intimate and global by the day. And that uplift is countered by the dissolution of myths that no longer serve us, and the demise of institutions that have underpinned our culture since the beginning of our

---

[20] Eckhart Tolle, *A New Earth: Awakening to Your Life's Purpose* (London: Penguin Books, 2005).

history. Our planetary world view is shifting to wide angle and refocusing its lens as we awaken to the reality of our interdependence.[21]

Conclusion

There is deep suspicion of a grand narrative (religious traditions, empires, capitalism, science, communism), because a grand narrative can become an ideology that can harden into legalism. Think of the implicit grand narratives proposed in presidential campaigns. We need to avoid narratives that promote the worth and value of one group of people over others.

We need to promote narratives that do not see civilization as a victory over nature. For example, in the last few years China has put forth a different, aspirational model of development—to become an "ecological civilization" rooted in Confucian concepts of harmonious environmental, material, social, and spiritual development. It is not clear what this means in practice, but it's an important opening to a new ecological narrative.

The wholeness and cycle of becoming models are not limited to a personal narrative or one dependent on the perspectives we bring to the process. The models incorporate the best of science (although not its philosophical materialism) and give us the tools to tell a new story in multiple ways from an integral view of science and religion.

As I have reflected on the theory and practice of catholicity presented in the four chapters of Part I, I turned to Matthew Fox's account of Meister Eckhart's contribution to the evolutionary journey. Fox says that we need to go beyond history. Eckhart takes us to the "edge of consciousness, the edge of chaos and order, the edge where creativity happens and where evolution can take new leaps of consciousness and action."[22]

---

[21] Jan Phillips, *No Ordinary Time: The Rise of Spiritual Intelligence and Evolutionary Creativity* (San Diego, CA: Living Kindness Foundation, 2011), 1.

[22] Matthew Fox, *Meister Eckhart: A Mystic Warrior for Our Times* (Novato, CA: New World Library, 2014), 274.

Eckhart and Fox describe the cycling to the bedrock and back to the surface this way:

> This is another way of saying that Eckhart insists that we do more than . . . rub the surface dimensions of culture and self; we must go *deeply* into them, to the edge of our understandings and experience. . . . We need to go down deep into the darkness, into the mystery, into the shadow, into the forgotten parts of ourselves as individuals and communities and as a species. . . . We must also surface. We must come back changed and ready to make change. . . . The future requires all of us to dive deep and return, surfacing with the wisdom, the mysteries, and the truths we learned from diving.[23]

---

[23] Ibid., 274–75.

Part II

Achieving Wholeness

The wholeness model and the cycle of becoming model presented in Part I are the foundation of a wholeness narrative about the three dimensions of body, mind, and soul. They are an interconnected dynamic wholeness of catholicity.

The models represent reality as we know it. Ultimate Reality, of course, is beyond our understanding. The models show the linkage and connectedness of everything in our diverse world— the physical, consciousness, and the spiritual. Each dimension of inquiry (body, mind, and soul) has its own language, epistemology, and ontology. The interactions can be seen at each stratum.

Our smaller, ego self tries to limit our access to deeper strata. It wants to remain at the surface, where it can keep control. In accepting and trusting the cycling process, we are connecting to the wisdom and love at the bedrock and the deep silence of the core.

Chapter 5, "Deep Identity," applies the models to individual self-development. Specific examples and methods of cycling through the middle stratum of emotions to the bedrock of the unconscious, dreams, and creative possibilities and back to the surface are presented. The goal is to let go of unfulfilling concerns to find the joy and inspiration of what we truly long for and get on with a purposeful life.

Chapter 6, "Deep Relationships," explores how we can develop greater relationships and values of empathy, giving, and cooperation. Difference, boundary, and inclusion issues can be resolved if we cycle through the strata of reality with others. Groups can identify the power and economic dynamics at the surface and discern what vision for greater social and political justice emerges from a journey to the bedrock.

Chapter 7, "Deep Ecology," focuses on how accessing deep levels of awareness of nature can change attitudes and behavior regarding climate change and our destruction of the biosphere.

Chapter 8, "Deep Moral Agency," focuses on how the energy and love at the bedrock is expressed through our actions. We all are role models with a responsibility for participating in the renewal of our communities, our work places, and our politics. Transformation of our purpose is possible by embracing what is stirring in the bedrock.

The essential message in the chapters in Part II is that we need to go deeper than the surface of our lives and societal norms to discover the bedrock source of our reality, whether we think of this as God, a sacred presence, or the ultimate mystery. Individually and collectively we can maintain the crucial connection to the bedrock. Life, consciousness, and the expression of our soul are dependent on the deep wisdom that resides there.

When we attend to this deep wisdom, we are coherent in a quantum sense, mindful, and in touch with inner divinity. As the cycle of becoming model illustrates, something new is always emerging from the bedrock. We surrender our own will and accept the inspiration that arises.

Chapter 5

Deep Identity

> *Our personality is vast and mysterious. Our inner world is like a universe, and the greatest adventure of life is to explore our inner worlds.*
>
> —Carl G. Jung,
> "The Development of Personality"

> *Don't ask what the world needs. Ask yourself what makes you come alive. Then go do it. Because what the world needs is more people who have come alive.*
>
> —Howard Thurman

Developing Self-Identity

Our sense of who we are—our self-identity—has many aspects. We have a sense of the body we animate. When we wake up, our mind tells us that we are different from the person in the dream world we were in. Religious experiences tell us that we are more than our body and mind, that we have a soul that is a transcendent reality beyond time and space.

The sense of who we are is constantly shifting as we cycle through the strata of the three dimensions of body, mind, and soul. Our recalled sense of who we were in the past, what is important to us in the here and now, and what we imagine for our future constantly changes. Yet all this awareness is tied into a coherent whole—our self-identity as a human being.

Many self-help books stress finding and reconnecting with your authentic self, to become who you really are. *Enlightenment* is the term that is traditionally used to denote "the unity of the individual self with ultimate reality." Enlightenment conveys a sense of freedom, fullness, and wholeness to the individual.[1]

Our self-identity is developed from our daily subjective experiences as we cycle through the levels of reality (surface, middle, and bedrock). "For the first time in humanity's history . . . humanity can train itself to be whole, to be unified, to be integrated, and not to be partial, fragmented and broken."[2] In this chapter I offer some ways to think about and influence that process.

Clarifying Values

Our larger or higher self is empowered and not restricted to the demands of the ego, our smaller self. The smaller self is focused on survival and security. For those acquainted with the Maslow hierarchy of values, the physiological needs of food, water, and sleep and the security needs of a home are core values of the smaller self. The values of social relationships—a sense of belonging, self-esteem, achievement, and recognition—are middle range values certainly important to having a good life. The larger self is driven by the top values of the hierarchy, a drive for self-actualization, serving others, and doing worthwhile things.

We have the capacity to transcend our material and social needs and values to achieve a larger self. Our most important values transcend the personal in service to something greater than ourself and to doing what is right, beautiful, true, and good. This is what gives us a sense of meaning and satisfaction.

To clarify our values, we must be vulnerable and surrender our attachment to the values prized by the smaller ego-driven

---

[1] Ken Wilber, *The Religion of Tomorrow* (Boulder, CO: Shambhala, 2017), 5.

[2] Ibid., 65.

self on the surface. Jesus became aware of his larger self, which Christians call the Christ, as did the Buddha, Saint Francis, the Dalai Lama, and others. We also have that capability.

The barrier to evolving a deeper self-identity is the culture of fear we live in. We cannot relax when our instincts are waging war, our minds are overloaded with information, and "we are chronically vigilant in a world we perceive is out to get us."[3] Fear is the antithesis of love.

Finding Deeper Self-Identity on the Surface

To pursue the good, true, and beautiful on the surface, we need to take in and synthesize information from multiple sources and continuously update our view of reality.

Our perceptions and intuitions are not the truth or ultimate Reality. We perceive and intuit things that fit what we need to survive. This is essential, especially when we need to make quick decisions, but these perceptions and intuitions may mean something more. We think we need to burn fossil fuel to survive—to keep us warm in the winter and cool in the summer. While this is "true," a deeper meaning is that it is changing our climate. To get to a deeper awareness of what we sense and intuit, we need to use multiple ways of knowing.

Accessing the wisdom of others, finding hard evidence, valuing our own intuitions, and relying on our own experience are four ways to arrive at a deeper understanding of any situation we face.

To be fully aware of the reality and meaning of any life situation, we need to use four ways of knowing (see Figure 5–1). They are authority, empiricism, insight, and praxis.[4] A reality-based deeper awareness arises from the interaction of these four ways of knowing. The model suggests that new knowledge emerges between any two ways of knowing and what can creatively emerge when all four ways interact. This model portrays what

---

[3] Bruce Sanguin, "What My New Puppy Has Taught Me—So Far," blog.

[4] Edwin E. Olson, *Finding Reality: Four Ways of Knowing* (Bloomington, IN: Archway Publishing, 2014).

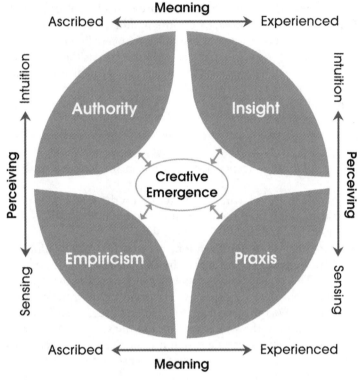

Figure 5–1. Ways of Knowing

is happening at one moment of time. The cycle of becoming suggests that through a succession of moments, our self-identity is created over time.

Authority

Much of our knowledge is derived from history, from things we have read, from parents, teachers, and the media. Many rely on information from "talking heads" on TV, Wikipedia, Google, and Facebook. Conventional wisdom, beliefs, and assumptions are passed along to us by many means.

This is obviously a good thing. The beliefs and assumptions of people across the world can inspire us to value peace, love, and justice. The problem is that, taken alone, some of the beliefs and faiths we have inherited and are exposed to daily can sadly inspire us to hate, discriminate, and wage war.

Faith in authority is necessary. Even scientists have faith in matters they have not directly observed or measured. We need the general sense of direction we glean from authority as we make decisions and go about our daily lives.

It is natural to want to believe in things people tell us, what we read, what is on TV, and what is on the Internet, but as we explore the other three ways of knowing, it is obvious that, standing alone, authority can give us an incorrect or limited interpretation about what is happening around us and in the world.

Empiricism

An empirical approach to knowledge asks one main question: What potential observational or experimental evidence do you have? Empirical evidence involves our five senses and tells us what of the material world can be seen, touched, smelled, heard, or tasted. We cannot see or touch gravity, but it is a natural law that can be experienced, tested, and predicted.

Science formulates theories that can explain the evidence yielded from the tools it uses to measure and quantify reality. As science progresses, it continually defines and refines theories if the data so require, creating new theories. Any given theory may not be the ultimate truth, but it serves as a useful approximation to the truth we need to understand and predict what happens in our world.

Like authority, an empirical way of knowing is a good thing. However, the modern era is overly enamored with empirical knowing. Empiricism is the modern equivalent of "having God on our side." It exerts such authority that we believe that to be taken seriously, we need empirical backing.[5] Empirical knowledge excels at explaining how things happen, but has no capacity for accessing the ultimate meaning of the vast collection of happenings we call "life."

[5] Bruce Sanguin, "Empiricism Has Replaced the Authority of Scriptures," blog.

Marcelo Gleiser calls the total of our accumulated knowledge the "Island of Knowledge" in a sea of mystery.[6] As the island expands, we have more questions and mysteries. To go beyond the boundaries of the island of empiricism, there are two additional ways of knowing: insight and praxis.

Insight

The accumulated wisdom of authority and the theories and evidence of empiricism expand our islands of knowledge, but, as individuals we contribute to that expansion through our personal intuition. Both Einstein and Newton used their intuition to speculate about the laws of the universe. Throughout history people have used their imagination to see beyond the occurrences in the everyday world. Our visions and insights are essential ways of knowing.

Insight is inherently mysterious. Thoughts, ideas, dreams, epiphanies, and hunches come to us, some based on our knowledge and experience, but some seemingly come from nowhere. Whether produced internally through meditation or brought to our awareness from outside sources, insights are provisional and fleeting, yet generative and often capable of putting authority and empiricism into a new perspective.

Praxis

Much in our lives keeps us from experiencing reality. We think about paddling a canoe, but this is different from the experience of being in a canoe. We read books and newspapers to tap into the newest ideas, discoveries, and events, but experiencing a reality we have read about is a different kind of knowing.

Praxis is the direct experience of life itself. We may tear up when we see something beautiful because we are "in" the experience. The essence of something is experienced in praxis. We are not fully aware of what war is until we fight in one, or of what it takes to paint a picture until we apply a brush to canvas.

---

[6] Marcelo Gleiser, *The Island of Knowledge: The Limits of Science and the Search for Meaning* (New York: Basic Books, 2014).

Being Aware with Four Ways of Knowing

The value and power of each way of knowing is impressive. It is obvious that we need to use all four ways, yet often we do not. When we idolize one or two ways of knowing, we give short shrift to the others, keep the different sources from interacting, and miss the larger reality.

When we grant absolute status to one or two ways of knowing and ignore the possibilities that can emerge from the interaction of the four ways of knowing, we do not see and participate in the wholeness of reality.

Superficial Identity

For many, life on the surface these days seems to be a series of phone calls, browsing the Internet, watching TV, listening to the radio while in a car, playing video games, and using an app on a smart phone, such as checking Twitter. With all the media devices around us, we have infinite ways to distract ourselves.

Dan Ariely, a behavior economist and expert on human irrationality, says that "modern temptations are killing us." When moments without stimulation arise, we start to feel panicked and don't know what to do with them, because we've trained ourselves to expect the stimulation of new notifications and alerts. "Our willpower diminishes the more we resist. . . . Rules are very useful to conserve willpower. Religion is a master of this art. By creating rules, it is easier to not even consider the temptation." To deal with the temptation of distractions and superficiality everywhere around us, we need to "create new rules and strategies to deal with it."[7]

Some of us are so identified with life on the surface that we feel threatened when our political or economic views are questioned, even resorting to violence to suppress the speech of others. When our self-identity is mostly tied to the conditions of life on the surface, when life goals seem unattainable, we become

---

[7] Dan Ariely, "Who Put the Monkey in the Driver's Seat?" lecture, Chautauqua, New York, Chautauqua Institution, July 20, 2015.

insecure and defensive, resenting "those who are perceived as outsiders."[8]

Our insecurities, our susceptibility to temptation, and the loss of introspection and the contemplative mind are strong arguments for developing rules and strategies that open our lives to opportunities to go deep to the bedrock. Some strategies are listed below. It will be helpful to reflect on your own strategies.

- Consciously create a pattern to your day to include space and time for what you want to happen.
- Take a pilgrimage or go on a retreat to experience something both physical and real.
- Befriend someone in a completely different socioeconomic category.
- Attend a different church, mosque, temple, or synagogue.
- Live substantially below your means.
- Travel to a different culture.
- Listen deeply to someone with completely different ideological beliefs and search for common ground.
- Work in a garden, vineyard, or on a farm.
- Go on a "technology fast" for a set period of time (hours to months).

Cycling to a Deeper Self-Identity

Cycling creates the conditions within ourselves for something new to emerge. From an evolutionary perspective the emergence of that which is new and enables us to live better is the greatest good. The challenge is to learn how to cycle effectively so that which is truly greater and new can emerge through us.

The creative impulse of evolution is already in the bedrock and core; cycling is not a matter of trying hard but of surrendering our egoic striving on the surface. We begin by staying alert to what our bodies are sensing, to what our intuition is telling us, and to the leading of Spirit. This is shifting from mere existence to conscious experience.

---

[8] Amanda Taub, "Behind the Gathering Turmoil, a Crisis of White Identity," *New York Times*, November 2, 2016, A6.

Cycling to a deeper self-identity means leaving behind those things that seemed at one point so central to our identity. What was once satisfying now seems partial and artificial. A longing is created for the next stage of our journey to a deeper identity.

When we are stuck on the surface, when we are living according to the dictates of our smaller self, the purpose of our larger self is not clear. Cycling brings us to the highest and deepest expression of what it means to be human.

Each of the nine parts of the wholeness model (Chapter 1) is connected to the whole. For example, I recently coped with limping because of a pain in my right hip. Several months of physical therapy had not helped. My left hip was replaced five years ago, so I knew that I was probably due for another replacement. As I reflected on my situation, I used the model to understand what was happening.

As I put the whole picture together in what is represented in Figure 5–2, I realized that my hip issue in the body dimension needed my time and attention. In the mind dimension I needed time to create the first draft of this book. In the soul dimension I

The Strata	Body	Mind	Soul
Surface	I am limited in my ability to walk. I try exercise, medication, therapy. It is getting worse.	I am in the process of writing this book, drawing upon several theories and apply a new theory.	I participate in and lead a study group at my church where we are reading new books on science and mysticism.
Middle	I notice where the pain is located and its connection to some lower backache.	I question whether the effort of writing the book is worth it. Do I really have something new and useful to say?	I meditate on the themes that have emerged from my reading and discussions at the church.
Bedrock	During an MRI procedure, I talk (silently) to the atoms in my hip and ask for a clear picture of what is going on.	I pay attention to my dreams and especially my lucid moments upon waking where it is clear why the book is important.	I trust "God" (my sense of God) for help in prioritizing my life, for giving me a big picture of how my life is moving forward.

Figure 5–2. Experiencing the Relationships in the Wholeness Model

reflected deeply on my priorities and discerned that finishing the first draft of this book was near the top of the list.

The three themes that emerged (physical health of my hip; time to write the book; and identifying my priorities) were all connected. More awareness and attention to each theme created clarity and a positive impact on the other two.

I decided to cancel my scheduled trip to the Institute on Religion in an Age of Science (IRAS) conference on Star Island, New Hampshire. This was a difficult decision because I was scheduled to deliver a paper and meet with distinguished scholars of the science-religion dialogue.

The exercise of documenting the process gave rise to new insights but also sharpened my day-to-day focus on priorities and generally had a calming effect as I knew that everything was working out.

After completing Figure 5–2, I was excited to see that my hip issues, book-writing task, and connection to fellow mystics and an inner guide were all synchronized and moving in the same direction on the surface.

My work on the book shifted into high gear, and I became more enthusiastic and committed. My priorities were clear. I balanced my time (in no particular order) between swimming, healthy eating, writing the book, spending time with Judith, and visiting my children.

(I did receive a hip replacement several months later. All is well.)

As I reflected further on my experience with my hip, I realized it was part of my continued journey from the smaller self to the larger self described by Sanguin.[9] Instead of blindly following my plans, I hesitated, admitting that I did not know what was best to do. Rather than seeing only the negative in the situation, I saw an embedded gift. I owned that my ego was a large part of the problem. As I moved from my smaller self on the surface to my larger holistic self, the middle and the bedrock had much to teach me. I shifted "from seeing through a lens of fragmentation and alienation to seeing the Wholeness that is animating and living all of my life."[10]

---

[9] Bruce Sanguin, *The Way of the Wind: The Path and Practice of Evolutionary Christian Mysticism* (Vancouver: Viriditas Press, 2015), 100.

[10] Ibid.

Contribution of the Middle to Deep Self-Identity

Our everyday lives may be filled with agitations, phobias, mood swings, and fears. In the face of such negativity and anxiety in the middle, we can find ways to remove ourselves from the immediacy of the experience. We can push aside our feelings with distractions. If we feel uncomfortable or unsafe, we fall into old patterns of behavior.

Or we may have pleasant emotions in the middle, such as joy, serenity, and peace, and mindlessly go with the flow of daily events. In either case we may be missing what is truly meaningful, something hidden in the ordinary that has a deeper meaning for us and others.

I have presented an optimistic and hopefully uplifting account of how the turbulence of the middle provides the impetus for movement both up to the surface and down to the bedrock and core. The turbulence and turmoil is similar in the three dimensions of the body, mind, and soul, at least metaphorically.

We must "dance" with the molecules, feelings, and meditation in the middle strata to reach coherence in the bedrock.

If we do not engage our turbulent emotions of fear, anxiety, envy, and so forth, we become locked into a cycle with the turmoil of our life on the surface and cannot get to the bedrock for liberation. Our anxiety and fears and our unexamined assumptions can control our life on the surface and keep us from changing, adapting, and becoming fully human. For example, if I feel rejected in the middle stratum because of rebuffs on the surface and conclude that I am not good enough, I act on the surface in ways that reinforce that cycle.

An acute loss creates intense emotions, such as grief, that destroy a person's inner sense of security. Grief is made up of a cluster of emotions—anger, fear, disappointment. By intentionally engaging in the grieving process, we are able to let go of these negative emotions and find peace and love at the bedrock

Anger is a healthy human emotion. It allows us to give voice to our grievances. Some anger can propel us to the surface to take appropriate action, but if we ruminate in anger, it debilitates us and we remain stuck in the middle.

Lisa Feldman Barrett, a professor of psychology at Northeastern University, says that if we consider negative emotions more precisely, we can develop "emotional granularity," which is the ability to differentiate between our emotions and the affect each is having on us. Developing this identity helps us to be more agile at regulating our emotions, less likely to drink when stressed, and less likely to retaliate aggressively against someone who has hurt us.[11]

> Perhaps surprisingly, the benefits of high emotional granularity are not only psychological. People who achieve it are also likely to have longer, healthier lives. They go to the doctor and use medication less frequently, and spend fewer days hospitalized for illness. Cancer patients, for example, have lower levels of harmful inflammation when they more frequently categorize, label and understand their emotions.

With higher emotional granularity, your brain may construct a more specific emotion, such as righteous indignation, which entails the possibility of specific actions. You are no longer an overwhelmed spectator but an active participant. You have choices. This flexibility ultimately reduces wear and tear on your body (e.g., unnecessary surges of cortisol).[12]

More finely tuned emotions keep us from continuous loops between the surface and the middle based on fear, anger, and the desire to control. To avoid being stuck in our superficial surface identity and in a loop of cycling to negative feelings in the middle stratum, we must cycle to the bedrock.

Cycling to the Bedrock

We do not find our deep identity solely in the neurochemicals of our body, or in our psyche that generates our images and symbols of our self, or in the reality of our spiritual experience. To find our deep personal identity, a holistic integration of the wisdom from the bedrock of all three dimensions is needed.

---

[11] Lisa Feldman Barrett, "The Benefits of Despair," *New York Times*, June 5, 2016, SR10.

[12] Ibid.

We need our physical instincts, our unconscious symbols, and the love of the Divine to reach our deep self. Avoiding any of the three dimensions can lead to onesidedness and "stuckness."

The process of individuation developed by Carl Jung is an effective way to think of developing a deep identity. In Jungian therapies, individuals transform by accessing their personal unconscious as well as the collective unconscious. The unconscious is filled with mythic images, a libido, preferences for extraversion and introversion, the healing and predictive functions of dreams, and the capacity to create fantasies and visions.

> Individuation appears, on the one hand, as the synthesis of a new unity which previously consisted of scattered particles, and on the other hand, as the revelation of something which existed before the ego and is in fact its father or creator and also its totality.[13]

The wisdom of the unconscious is brought into the consciousness of our personality. The psyche becomes integrated and the process has a holistic healing effect on the person, both mentally and physically.

If it is so wonderful, why is the individuation process consciously undertaken by relatively few?

> Self-recollection, however, is about the hardest and most repellent thing there is for man, who is predominantly unconscious. Human nature has an invincible dread of becoming more conscious of itself. What nevertheless drives us to it is the Self.[14]

Later in this chapter I discuss four practical methods for engaging in the individuation process—journaling, deep prayer, mindful meditation, and active imagination.

---

[13] C. G. Jung, "Individuation," *Collected Works*, vol. 11 (Princeton, NJ: Princeton University Press, 2000), 23.

[14] Ibid.

Achieving Coherence

Cycling through the strata of surface, middle, and bedrock and to the core develops coherence at a deep level: from this comes deep wisdom and understanding. For example, while writing this book, I had this dream:

> I am at a Gestalt conference. I had been attending many of the lectures. At one session after the lecture a woman asked me to move. I had talked about the importance of quantum biology. As we started moving, everything became aligned and I start to float around the room. Everyone was amazed. The temperature needs to be 120 degrees.[15] I tell people I am in a coherent state, there is no time. After, I didn't feel the pain in my hip, even when I woke up. I didn't think I was dreaming. It was real. I told people this was important. I demanded they pay attention. I was in dreamtime. It started with movement. I told people I was in coherence. The trigger was a figure, a half-circle. When I touched it, I went into coherence.

The dream can be interpreted in many ways. Regarding deep self-identity, the dream emphasizes the impact of achieving a deep level of internal coherence. Coherence, as explained by the quantum biologists, is that state in the bedrock of living cells where the quantum possibilities—electrons being everywhere at once—create instant transformations.

In developing the larger self we can transcend the limits we have imposed on ourselves. Although the dream indicated that even levitation is possible, the reality of internal coherence did affect my feelings and even the pain in my hip. It felt real. That I triggered coherence in the dream by touching something was interesting. In the field of neuro-linguistic programming, one technique is to associate touching one area of the body with transporting the person to a blissful place.

---

[15] In one belief system I discovered on the Internet, (0) cipher is the completion of a circle consisting of 360 degrees (120 degrees of knowledge, 120 degrees of wisdom, and 120 degrees of understanding), which is a whole.

That the setting for the dream was a Gestalt conference is significant. Gestalt psychology is all about wholeness, the theme of this book. The importance of movement in the dream suggests cycling through the strata of reality. My sense that there was no time suggests I was in the bedrock. Just as quantum particles have no boundaries and are everywhere at once, it makes sense that I could float around the room.

Coherence isn't possible if we are distracted from our experience in the moment. Being fully present to what is before us requires inhabiting the present moment with full attention and engagement. Coherence is the small miracle that emerges.

To attain a level of coherence that will make a difference, we need to go to the bedrock to accept our limitations, to find the humility and the deep trust that God is present in what we cannot change.

Finding Deep Self-Identity in the Bedrock and Core

The bedrock is the generative force of the universe. All things come into existence and then dissolve back into the Great Mystery of the bedrock and core. Paradoxically, moving to the bedrock sustains and produces new life but it also involves a death—a death of the excesses of the ego. Jung said that a blow to the ego is a victory for the larger self. Ironically, if we defeat the ego, we defeat death. Our transformation in developing a deeper identity requires death for the new to be born.

An extensive journey to the bedrock often begins when a person is stuck in his or her life experiences by some irresolvable crisis. When life on the surface becomes difficult, some aspects of the personality and psychological functions that have been neglected or repressed and reside in the bedrock may be activated. The crisis exposes what Jung called the "shadow" and presents an opportunity for personal growth (individuation).

Dreams, which are important vehicles for personal growth, can be unsettling. Throughout history many have believed that an external god was communicating with them through dreams. Jung initially found these godlike archetypes irritating:

Archetypes speak the language of high rhetoric, even of bombast. It is a style I find embarrassing; it grates on my nerves, as when someone draws his nails down a plaster wall, or scrapes his knife against a plate.[16]

But it is exactly that irritating quality that indicates that you are indeed tapping truly unconscious material at the bedrock.

Going to the bedrock and core can be scary. Letting go of attachments on the surface and negative emotions in the middle and deeply evaluating and reflecting on what we did and need to do are difficult.

But when we get to the bedrock and core, in the dark we find the light of God and the source of happiness, empathy, joy, and peace. The bedrock is like a deep well gushing forth living waters. If we stay connected, the coherence in the bedrock will flow to our life in the world. God, the self-organizing process in the universe, is always getting us to pause in order to teach, lure, and even compel us into the future.

Why don't we descend to the bedrock and core all the time? Because we have well-defined mechanisms for surviving in the world. We make observations, we collapse the waves of possibility, we kill coherence. We confront the mysterious, wild world of spirit and map it, flatten it, and define it within a quantified, operationalized regime of control.

We regularly disrupt the coherence that lets God speak to us, that makes our souls receptive to love, that makes mystery potent. When we break that coherence, we live in fear, we create stress for ourselves and others, and ultimately our soul becomes sick. Breaking that coherence can even manifest in physical symptoms.

It is a good thing to snap out of reverie and take immediate action when we are faced with a danger, but not when we want the wisdom that lies deep in the bedrock and core. Like the metaphor of photons tunneling through the barriers in living cells, the Spirit tunnels through the three strata of existence when we are open to it and don't try to control it.

---

[16] C. G. Jung, *Memories, Dreams, Reflections* (New York: Vintage Books, 1989 <1961>).

Methods for Exploring Self-Identity

There are many ways and paths to self-enlightenment. Many of the readers of this book have doubtless read many books on self-improvement and attended workshops and retreats on how to journey deep within to experience the Divine and develop greater spiritual intelligence. In the context of the wholeness model, cycling to our inner spiritual life, our bedrock, informs our outer journey on the surface.

Here are some ways to prepare for an inner journey; you may have preparations that are comparable:

- Listen to calming music.
- Read scripture and inspirational books.
- Listen to sermons and inspirational talks.
- Use incense and aroma therapy.
- Look at the night sky or the Hubble images of the universe.
- Sit on the beach, in the woods, or in a boat on a lake.
- Touch a sculpture or gaze at an icon.
- Read or write a poem.
- Work with clay or paint.
- Watch the sun or moon rise or set.
- Float in an outdoor pool and study the clouds.

In choosing a method for an inner journey, we can *replicate* what we have done before that was successful and meaningful. But at times we need to *innovate* and do something new to create new spiritual pathways.

When our lives are stable we often *replicate*—do what is predictable, what is reliable, what we have confidence in, what we usually do. This is a good thing, but the problem is that these practices can become boring or even limiting. We may stop even expecting anything new to happen.

When our lives are unstable; when we are depressed; when we experience the stress of illness; when friends or family leave us; when we have financial problems, and so on—we need to *innovate*. We need to take actions that are unpredictable, creative, surprising, challenging, and exciting. We need a new thing.

Exploring a deeper self-identity with the wholeness model can enhance most methods used to journey inward. I illustrate this with the most common methods—journaling, deep prayer, mindful meditation, and active imagination.

Journaling

By regularly writing down the insights that emerge from the bedrock, we can better understand our moods generated by the turbulent emotions in the middle stratum. We also can clarify why we behave as we do on the surface. Drawing images of what we experience in dreams or in our daily lives can move us beyond analytical, rational thinking to compassionate understanding and wisdom.

Even if you don't feel like it, write anyway. Just start writing in a "stream of consciousness" without judgment, editing, censoring your thoughts, or correcting your grammar.

The wholeness model can be helpful in organizing the images, insights, and thoughts. In reviewing my journal, I make a notation of the stratum the entry has evoked: surface (S), middle (M), or bedrock (B).

For example, if I notice something in the natural world that I experience as magical or mysterious, I record "B" for bedrock. When a song triggers a strong memory, I write down how I felt then and how I feel now and record "M" for middle. If I have a question or concern, I mark it "S" for surface and wait for a response to come from the bedrock.

By reflecting on the strata of my journal entries I am more conscious of the cycling process and my self-development.

Deep Prayer

> Prayer is the awakening of the mind to God. . . . To pray is . . . to retreat from the frenzy of life and to center the heart on God. . . . Prayer is centering the mind on ultimate life-energy—God—through which we are connected to the entire universe. It opens the heart to a greater fullness of life and challenges us to surrender those parts of ourselves that we find unlovable or try to control or manipulate.[17]

[17] Ilia Delio, *Making All Things New: Catholicity, Cosmology, Consciousness* (Maryknoll, NY: Orbis Books, 2015), 169–71.

For Richard Rohr, prayer means "any interior journey or practice that allows you to experience faith, hope, and love within yourself."[18]

When I pray I sense a deep and overwhelming awareness of inner power and light. This awareness comes from being connected to the bedrock and to the core energy that flows through the universe.

The goal of prayer with the cycle of becoming is to apprehend the ultimate nonsensuous unity in all things, a oneness neither the senses nor the reason can penetrate. We start with a mystical experience of the external world at the surface. This is the same One that we find in the depths of the self at the core. The Divine is already indwelling and at work in ways we do not comprehend. Our prayer's purpose is to realize or reaffirm our true identity as both human and divine. It is distinguishing our ego-self and our deep identity, our soul, our indwelling divine immanence that permeates or infuses the cosmos.

Prayer reduces the turbulence in the middle stratum, calms the ego on the surface, and creates coherence in the bedrock. The dynamic and constantly circulating prayer energy at the bedrock level is the Spirit at work—doing two or a hundred things at once, affecting things faster than the speed of light, and passing through impenetrable barriers. Going to the bedrock establishes coherence with the highest, deepest, and most encompassing reality that religions call God. A mystic prayer: "Draw me unto Thee, O my Divine centre, by the secret springs of my existence, and all my powers and senses shall follow the potent magnetism!"[19]

In the mystic prayer the magnetism of the Divine in creating bedrock coherence is analogous to the powerful magnets in an MRI machine that align the hydrogen atoms in our body. The divine-in-us is our own magnet.

Finding time for silence and solitude during the day, even for a period of two minutes, helps us to center ourselves, to know who we are, and to move into the day with a sense of our true identity.

---

[18] Richard Rohr, "Daily Meditation Contemplation: The Inner Witness," blog, February 2, 2017.

[19] "A Short and Easy Method of Prayer—Chapter 21," A Reasonable Mystic blog, November 26, 2008, http://www.reasonablemystic.com.

Mindful Meditation

The growth of mindfulness meditation in the United States is about a longing to find a meaningful response to the overwhelming complexity of our lives. In meditation we can put away some of the trivial concerns and pay attention to what is truly important.

In meditation we can observe how easily our minds jump from one thought to the other on the surface. As meditation continues, our sensations, emotions, and feelings from the middle emerge. As we let them go, the stillness and serenity of the bedrock takes over and we develop resilience to recover from the setbacks in our life.[20]

Saint John of the Cross likened meditation to being logs in a fireplace. The log of wood gradually becomes transformed in fire and at last takes on the fire's own properties.[21] These properties are an expression of God's energy within.

Active Imagination

As an adjunct to his work with dreams, Carl Jung developed a technique he called active imagination that facilitated an inward journey. Active imagination is a process of consciously dialoguing with our unconscious.

As in prayer and meditation, the practice of active imagination is receptive to whatever the bedrock produces, but "unlike prayer and meditation, a person can react with conscious intent by engaging in a dialogue with the image of the person or object that has emerged."[22]

My own practice is to sit at my computer, slow my breathing, and quiet my mind as much as I can. I then type a question to,

---

[20] Richard J. Davidson and Sharon Begley, *The Emotional Life of Your Brain* (New York: Hudson Street Press, 2012).

[21] Saint John of the Cross, *Dark Night of the Soul*, bk. II, chap. xi, sect. 1, trans. and ed. E. Allison Peers from the critical edition of P. Silverio De Santa Teresa. CD electronic edition ed. Harry Plantinga. The text is in the public domain.

[22] Janet Dallett, "Active Imagination," in *Jungian Analysis*, ed. Murray Stein (LaSalle, IL: Open Court, 1982).

for example, an imaginal figure from a recent dream. Having begun the dialogue, I remain receptive to whatever emerges from within and simply type what comes out. After allowing the inner voice to speak as long as it likes, I shift back to my ego consciousness and react to what has been said. The dialogue continues in that manner.

I believe that what arises from the unconscious during my practice of active imagination is from the bedrock, forms my thoughts and feelings in the middle, and finally is expressed on the surface by my writing. Jung experienced his encounter with the unconscious and his negative feelings this way:

> Sometimes it was as if I were hearing it with my ears, sometimes feeling it with my mouth, as if my tongue were formulating words; now and then I heard myself whispering aloud. Below the threshold of consciousness everything was seething with life.
>
> One of the greatest difficulties for me lay in dealing with my negative feelings. I was voluntarily submitting myself to emotions of which I could not really approve, and I was writing down fantasies which often struck me as nonsense, and toward which I had strong resistances.[23]

One way I ground this process is to record the active imagination experience in my journal so that I can refer to it. In times of transition or difficulty, active imagination is an incredibly powerful method for gaining access to the information and love unavailable to consciousness.

When we hold the polarities of our conscious mind and what our dreams and intuitions are telling us, there is a shift in our psyche that moves us from one position to another. Differences in perspectives are reconciled. Exemplars like Jesus lived out what emerged for them from the tension between conscious and unconscious.

Jung said that when we are conscious of our negative feelings and emotions, we can turn them into an image that will reduce their oppressive impact. Focusing on his dark moods and

---

[23] Jung, *Memories, Dreams, Reflections*, 178.

transforming them into inner images saved Jung from thinking he was crazy.[24]

Conclusion

As we develop a deeper identity, we are in touch with an underlying dynamic of possibilities and connections. Small miracles happen, new discoveries are made, and creative solutions become apparent.

The entanglement at the quantum level, in the firing of millions of neurons in our brains, and the awesome embrace of the Spirit in the bedrock lead us in unforeseen directions. Healing occurs, hurts are forgiven, and constraints are thrown off.

In the process we can also be overwhelmed by the negative emotion and turbulence in the middle. We must remember to "dance" with the forces, or we will cut our connection to the possibilities, coherence, love, spirit, and self-transcendence at the bedrock.

In choosing to love and find love, to be instruments of peace in our minds and hearts and with our fellow beings, we create our heaven on earth. To reject the journey inward creates our own hell.

---

[24] Ibid.

Chapter 6

Deep Relationships

In cycling deep to the bedrock or core, as we saw in Chapter 5, we improve our physical, mental, and spiritual well-being, and we also improve our relationships with other humans and, indeed, all living beings. If we can include others with us on our journey, so much the better for both us and them.

Relationships constitute the whole, which is greater than any of its parts, but to function well, the whole needs to care for its parts, the relationships within. We see this in ecosystems where the complex webs of relationships among the species within the ecosystem are cared for by the whole system. In a healthy group or organization the relationships within have healthy interpersonal synergistic relationships.

In this chapter our quest for deeper synergistic relationships is seen as a means for continued self and communal development. By overcoming stereotypes and valuing differences, we can develop rich dialogues, compassion, and greater social justice as we help others.

Barriers to Deep Relationships

As we enter various circumstances, we often have a made-up mind. Our moral codes and traditions and our awareness of what has worked for us in the past usually dictate how we will behave. In short, our persona, how we present ourselves in the world, governs what we think is right and wrong. Bruce Sanguin says:

> The mind of ego loves fairness, tit for tat decision-making, meritocracy, comparing ourselves to others. It loves knowing that I am better than, more accomplished, faster than . . . somebody. Conversely, the mind of ego loves to prove that I am a nobody. It can spend an inordinate amount of time proving to the world that there is something intrinsically wrong with me. The mind of ego loves to separate and be separated.[1]

We also have ambiguous, often-conflicted responses to the possibility of intimacy in interpersonal relationships. Too often we project our anxieties and fears onto the other. We do this out of insecurity and uncertainty about whether we want to, or are capable of, being vulnerable to another.

Our ego helps us to cope with the everyday flow of situations we encounter by keeping things in order and under control. But to engage with others at a deeper level, we need to go to the bedrock to truly understand and connect with other people.

Our intimate, deep relationships with others and the natural world have also been diminished by technology.

By substituting virtual reality for face-to-face interaction, we do increase the number of people in our networks, but we reduce the breath and depths of intimate interactions. Our contacts and even our friends are reduced to a short text or photo without the emotional and soulful moments of our lives and their lives. As contacts, we present a superficial caricature of who we are and flatten our range of emotional experiences. We are tempted to focus on online life, because it is fun and diverting, but the cost is unsatisfying shallow relationships. A modern version of spiritual discipline along the lines of fasting is "regaining control of social impulses, saying no to a thousand shallow contacts for the sake of a few daring plunges."[2]

---

[1] Bruce Sanguin, "Made up Minds and the Mind of Christ," blog.

[2] David Brooks, "Intimacy for the Avoidant," *New York Times,* October 7, 2016, A27.

Relationships Develop the Self

When we pause and consider the many people we contact daily, we see that our lives are filled with relationships. Each relationship, when combined with others, adds a color, richness, and dimension to life that we could never experience without it. Each relationship gives us an opportunity to learn more about our authentic self and the role others play in shaping our identity. Our relationships are the vehicles for our evolution as individuals and a species.

Figure 6–1 illustrates how we can move from a fragmented, purposeless life at the surface, face our feelings of alienation, and go to the bedrock to find a sense of being whole and a connection that can propel us to finding relationships and living purposefully.

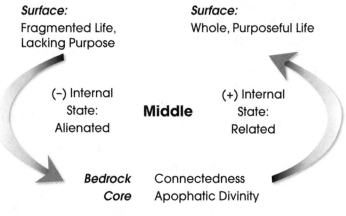

Figure 6–1. Cycle of Relationships

Everything we hold to be real, rational, and valuable depends on the well-being of our relationships. It is out of relationship that our individual identity emerges.[3]

---

[3] Kenneth J. Gergen, *Relational Being: Beyond Self and Community* (New York: Oxford University Press, 2009).

Reconciling with the "Other"

If our smaller self and obsession with superficial connections on the surface keep us from developing deep relationships with others, we are in danger of projecting our shadow onto others. If we don't acknowledge our own negative and ugly characteristics, we will see these characteristics in others, especially in times of political tensions and war. As the old saying goes, What we don't like about others is a reflection of what we don't like about ourselves.

If we feel things are falling apart, we may project the feeling on the "other" and think that the other is doing this to us. We attack our friends and partners for feelings that we pick up from them, but it is likely that something from our own shadow is making us feel bad, not the other person.

By moving from the ego on the surface and going to the unexplored aspects of our own bedrock we are likely to see the other's point of view. At this deep level we can develop empathy, experience the world from the other's point of view, and recognize other forces affecting relationships that are in the bedrock. We need to put the conscious and unconscious aspects of the situation in communication with each other. If we don't, they will lie on the surface through projections. By holding the contrasting images in tension, something else will emerge: transformation.

A common cause of our conflicts is the belief that we have been wronged or betrayed by the other. To reconcile and develop a deep relationship, we must forgive. We must recognize that our distress is from the hurt feelings and physical upsets we are experiencing in the moment, not from what has offended us in the past. Focusing on the moment and going to the bedrock to find a deeper connection to the person will help us to realize the feeling about the offenses we are experiencing are also shared by the other. We then have the opportunity to create the conditions where the offender can also participate by confessing to the wrong we experienced.

If both parties can descend to the bedrock and deal with the hard questions about the offense and the grievance, this opens the possibility of reconciling and rebuilding a new level of trust.

Dialogue to Deeper Relationships

To go deeper into our relationships on the surface and get to the troubling negative emotion in the middle as we open to the wisdom of the bedrock, we need to be in a dialogue of inquiry, not judgment.

Rather than proselytize, convincing others of our views, our goal is to establish a relationship of mutual respect and curiosity.

In a dialogue of inquiry, diversity of views can make the relationship more nuanced and exciting. As the parties to the dialogue listen deeply, a broader perspective and understanding can emerge. New channels and pathways are opened and an inclusive vision is possible.

Inquiry turns judgment into curiosity, disagreement into shared exploration, defensiveness into self-reflection, and assumptions into questions. By exploring mutual expectations and identifying options, the relationship can move forward or go deeper.

In preparation for a deep dive to the bedrock, it is important to create a safe place on the surface. Here are some useful guides for inviting others to explore the issue within a given time, with rules for authentic revelation and compassionate listening, where all are feeling powerful and in control and ready to listen to different views:

- Be sensitive to differences in communications.
- Avoid blaming.
- Pause before speaking, examining your own assumptions and perceptions.
- Trust the ambiguity in the dialogue.
- Promise confidentiality.
- Avoid trying to be "right" and making the other person "wrong."

Following these guides will facilitate going through the ambiguous and emotional middle to reach the grace at the bedrock. Under these conditions the quantum consciousness and spirit can do their work.

Martin Buber, a twentieth-century Jewish theologian who "dedicated his career to understanding deep intimacy . . . is famous for the distinction between I-It relationships and I-Thou relationships."[4] Buber explains that the "I" only exists in relation to some other. All through life the self is emerging out of some dialogue, either one that stifles development or one, as Ilia Delio states, that makes "each 'I' a living 'Thou' with a distinct personality."[5]

In I-Thou relationships nothing is held back. Deep questions can be asked with the expectation of heartfelt answers. For example, gazing into another's eyes can create coherence that makes possible the impossible, such as loving our enemies.

When we are invited into the spiritual realm of the other in the bedrock, we co-create meaning, understanding, and expression of these new perspectives at the surface. Although each may use a different language, symbol, or metaphor, both parties are expressing the same beliefs and goals on the surface.

Our commonly agreed-upon view of reality is in fact a shared set of assumptions or perceptions that we have mutually created. You and I develop a consensus on what is "out there" and experience it as objective reality.

Compassion

Empathy is feeling the pain of others. Compassion is being motivated and actively concerned about that pain. At the bedrock we see the deep connection between the pain of others and ourselves. To have an impact, we need to transform empathy into compassion and compassion into action on the surface.

When we bring this compassion to the surface, we extend our forgiveness for the slights and angry outbursts we experience from others. Because we have dealt with our own shortcomings while in the bedrock, we can understand even the violent actions of others.

The ability to be compassionate was an evolutionary competitive advantage for Homo sapiens. According to many anthropologists, taking care and protecting fellow humans when

---

[4] David Brooks, "Read Buber, Not the Polls," *New York Times*, November 1, 2016, A27.

[5] Ilia Delio, *The Unbearable Wholeness of Being: God, Evolution, and the Power of Love* (Maryknoll, NY: NJ: Orbis Books, 2013), 133.

they were ill or disabled helped our branch of early humans to survive while other humanoids failed to develop group cohesion and trust. "Parental affection ensured the survival of the species, helping the young to thrive, and taught humans to develop other alliances and friendships that were extremely useful in the struggle for survival. Gradually they developed the capacity for altruism."[6]

Although many animals demonstrate altruism, humans are by far the most empathic species on the planet, including recognizing that others have the same feelings as do we. Our mirror neurons sense the inner thoughts and expected actions of another person.[7]

Inspired by Wordsworth, Armstrong says "we can all create 'spots of time' for others, and that many of these will be the little, nameless, unremembered, acts of kindness and of love that Wordsworth claimed . . . form that best portion of a good man's life."[8] We can make daily resolutions to act in accordance with the Golden Rule and to channel our negative energy into a kindlier direction.[9]

We continue to develop our capacity for compassion by cycling to the bedrock and core where we find that God's Love-Energy is compassion, loving into being that which, as yet, does not exist. "Divine Love-Energy sees the potential, the possible beauty of what could be and calls it into being."[10] This essentially is quantum possibilities being manifested into human behavior. This deep compassion builds upon the awakening powers of attentive presence, intuitive listening and reverence.

As love becomes part of our spiritual practice, we can open ourselves up to the core, where we surrender and are completely

---

[6] Karen Armstrong, *Twelve Steps to a Compassionate Life* (New York: Anchor Books, 2010), 18.

[7] Empathy is made possible by a special group of nerve cells, called mirror neurons, at various locations inside the brain. These special cells enable us to "mirror" emotions.

[8] Armstrong, *Twelve Steps to a Compassionate Life,* 112.

[9] Ibid., 114.

[10] Francis Rothluebber, *Who Creates the Future: Discovering the Essential Energy of Co-Creation* (Idyllwild, CA: Womanspace, 2016), 74.

vulnerable and receptive to the Divine that is beckoning to us. At a TED conference in Vancouver, British Columbia,

> Pope Francis urged an audience of technophiles and entre-preneurs . . . to use their powers of curiosity and inquiry to explore and nurture the relationships that bond human beings to one another. "How wonderful would it be if the growth of scientific and technological innovation would come along with more equality and social inclusion. . . . How wonderful would it be, while we discover faraway planets, to rediscover the needs of the brothers and sisters orbiting around us."[11]

The pope's hope can come to fruition if we bring the love from the bedrock to the surface to learn about the suffering of others, listen to stories of sacrifice, serve and provide comfort to others, and further develop our empathy and compassion.

Developing Relationships by Helping Others

I had this dream on January 10, 2017:

> I am depressed and down on my luck. A young woman takes me to a place where people are rehabilitated. I gain strength. Later both the young woman and a middle-aged woman are available to be associated or married to me. I choose the middle-aged woman rather than the more at-tractive younger woman.

I believe this dream is an example of cycling to develop relation-ships that help others develop their full human potential. As I reflected on how I gained strength in the dream, I considered how I am able to go to deeper levels to help others. I recalled my study group at church where I meet with several senior women and men. I had been helping the group to study Mary Harrell's

---

[11] Pope Francis, reported in Russell Goldman, "Pope Tells Technology Leaders to Nurture Ties with Others," *New York Times*, April 27, 2017, A4.

book *Imaginal Figures in Everyday Life*.[12] In encouraging the women in the group to claim their "Crone" status,[13] my relationship with some of the women in the group deepened.

The fact that in the dream I chose one of the senior women to marry rather than a younger, more physically attractive woman, suggests that I also have developed greater maturity.

Through prayer, discernment, hospitality, service to others, forgiveness, testimony, dialogue, and friendship we create new connections. We affect the unconscious of others all the time and vice-versa. We communicate profoundly at unconscious levels. These deep connections wake us up to see ourselves, our neighbors, and our world from a different perspective. We awaken our imagination in the bedrock toward what might be, instead of only what was.

By reducing the turbulence between the surface and the bedrock, we calm the ego, which wants to control things, and we create coherence in the bedrock. The dynamic and constantly circulating energy at the bedrock stratum is the Spirit at work—doing two or a hundred things at once, affecting things faster than the speed of light, and passing through impenetrable barriers.

In conversations and group participation we reorganize consciousness and create coherence in ourselves and in others.

Developing Communal Identity

Developing deep interpersonal relationships is enhanced by working together on a common project. By working together to improve the lives of the disadvantaged, for example, the social distance between us and others will decrease.

Sanguin writes:

> Being a community is hard work—it is decidedly unnatural in our highly individualistic culture. Unless people get

---

[12] Mary Harrell, *Imaginal Figures in Everyday Life: Stories from the World between Matter and Mind* (Asheville, NC: InnerQuest Books, 2015).

[13] Ibid., 92. The Crone archetype is the face of the feminine that can best be described as a woman of age, power, and wisdom.

intentional about making themselves fit for community, it's not going to happen. This involves emotional and psychological healing as well as soul-work. Forget about soul-work or spiritual practice if people aren't willing to do emotional and psychological healing[14]

For authentic communication to arise, people need to do the hard work of dealing with the turbulent, troubling emotions that may be in the group (the middle) before they can get to the soul work in the bedrock that will propel them to spiritual practice on the surface.

In working with groups I have found that using the group sand tray method helps to create a strong group bond as well as evoking a deep sense of empowerment for the individual and the group.[15] For example, in one session I asked members of a church planning group to think about their life together in the next five years. To convey their vision, the members selected from a variety of symbols and placed them in the sand tray. As the members shared their stories and feelings with the rest of the group, a climate of trust was nurtured that enabled them to engage one another, appreciate their differences, and affirm their commonalities.

In multicultural groups representing a variety of identity groups, the sand tray symbols provide an innovative means for exposing and examining taken-for-granted value systems,

---

[14] Bruce Sanguin, "Community—What Is It and How Do We Get Fit for It. Part I," blog.

[15] Group sand tray is a process of discovery and contemplation as members listen to one another. After setting a general objective or theme, three to eight members go into a room with many shelves filled with small objects representing all facets of life, including those we can only imagine (such as dragons, ghosts). Members are encouraged to let their unconscious mind guide them in selecting objects by taking those items they are attracted to, even though they may not know what attracted them. A person may choose one, two, or several symbols. Members then place the objects in a large, round (five-foot diameter) tray filled with sand. They then sit around the tray and arrange their items, contemplate, and take turns sharing what the objects mean to them (Edwin E. Olson, "Using Imagery and Symbols in Organization Change," OD Practitioner 37, no. 3 [2005]: 23–28).

personal epistemologies, and stereotypes members bring to the group sessions. They also function to bring forth the richness and legitimacy of the members' values. Using the symbols, members experienced greater awareness of the lenses through which they and others view and understand the group they are evolving.

When communal identity is successfully developed, a group develops a "we" consciousness. People in the group love one another, so the good of the group comes first and the needs of the individuals are second. Together they sense a larger purpose and become co-creators of a new future.

Social Justice

For most of the 1990s, I worked as a diversity trainer and consultant to corporations and government agencies. The focus of the work was on valuing diversity, helping managers and employees to see differences in the work place as a positive feature. I provided many examples and led discussions on how diversity provides meaning and motivates action. Unless appreciated and valued, however, diversity can be divisive.

The goal of the training was to foster an understanding of diversity in order to drive the growth and health of the organization, not personal development per se. The organizations were willing to spend thousands of dollars to make that happen.

The most significant differences we worked with were race and gender. Other differences that arose were also included, especially age, physical and mental differences, and religion. In later years organizations became more willing to include sexual orientation in the training.

The training had varying degrees of success. Often it was initiated because of discrimination lawsuits, and the employees undergoing the training would often start out asking, "Why me? I had nothing to do with the problem." In most cases, at the end of the training, the participants saw the value of developing a more inclusive work place.

The most difficult issue was race, given our country's long history of racism, both personal and institutional. We were most successful when white participants were willing to confront their culture of white privilege and supremacy—in themselves and the organization. We were able to go to that level of awareness only by taking the participants to the bedrock of love. Through both videos and mixed-race group dialogues, whites could see that their myth of white innocence was a burden to themselves and the organization. They were able to look into the eyes of their colleagues and wake from their ignorance of what it meant to be a person of color in their organization. The dominant majority members of a group were able to understand the anxiety of the minority members, who continually have to "code-switch" to cope in their daily lives.[16]

A profound experience occurred in a diversity program in a federal government agency. My colleagues and I were called in by the human resource manager, who told us that after waking up in a sweat after a dream in which he was punishing blacks in the agency, he initiated the diversity program. It was a clear example of the deep stirring at the bedrock that can bring about dramatic personal transformation, and, in this instance, transformation in a work place.

I believe the human resource manager found God's love in the bedrock, the union of opposites, the potential for change, the illuminative source and strength of creativity. By cycling, the manager constructively opened the boundaries between his life on the surface and the bedrock. In doing so, he found the coherence and lure of what is needed for the future.

Coherence in one dimension of body, mind, and soul generates coherence for the whole. At the same time, coherence of the whole generates coherence in all the dimensions. If we want to achieve greater social justice in our organizations and in our country, then interactions among all of us, all the time, must be inspired by constructive use of difference. When an epidemic such as Ebola begins, it is difficult for individual people to follow the precautions well enough to avoid infection. When a larger percentage of the affected group understands and follows precautions, the epidemic ends. If that larger group never forms,

---

[16] Code-switching is modifying one's behavior, appearance, language, mannerisms, and so on, to adapt to different sociocultural norms, for example, using different languages at home and at work. Female Muslims must code-switch in going to places that require forgoing the hijab.

however, the infection runs rampant. As with viruses, so with social ills.

Consistently dealing with divisive differences among body, mind, and soul in ourselves and with others ultimately transforms differences in the whole.

Most of the differences that fuel the unsustainability we experience on the surface are caused by our tendency to reduce people to a single identity that blocks the empathy, love, and creative imagination we find in the bedrock. Such common simplified identities include black, white, Jewish, Muslim, Christian, elite, people, evangelical, Democrat, Republican. We voluntarily accept these simplistic tribal identities and use them to define how we see reality. David Brooks writes:

> Crude tribal dividing lines inevitably arouse a besieged, victimized us/them mentality. This mentality assumes that the relations between groups are zero sum and antagonistic. People with this mentality tolerate dishonesty, misogyny and terrorism on their own side because all morality lays down before the tribal imperative.
>
> The only way out of this mess is to continually remind ourselves that each human is a conglomeration of identities: ethnic, racial, professional, geographic, religious and so on. Even each identity itself is not one thing but a tradition of debate about the meaning of that identity. Furthermore, the dignity of each person is not found in the racial or ethnic category that each has inherited, but in the moral commitments that each individual has chosen and lived out.[17]

To reduce the impact of these differences on the surface, we must realize that each of us is a whole with many facets. Telling our stories about when we were oppressed or admitting to times when we were the oppressor is most possible when we are at the bedrock.

The bedrock produces patterns within patterns, the whole. Our tribal identity prevents us from seeing and participating in the wholeness because we grant absolute status to the part,

---

[17] David Brooks, "Danger of a Dominant Identity," *New York Times,* November 18, 2016, A31.

our tribe, rather than the wholeness. By being satisfied with the wholeness of our tribe, our traditions, our religion, we miss the greater whole that is in the bedrock.

Conclusion

By going to the bedrock, we overcome the constraints of our smaller self and deepen our relationships as others help us to know our own deep identity—our true self.

Stereotypes and superficial relationships at the surface, fostered by our use of social media, are barriers to developing a whole and purposeful life. Our culture of fear needs to be replaced by a culture of love in order to reconcile with those we project as our enemy and develop compassionate and helping relationships based on a dialogue of inquiry.

Continuing that process leads us to I-Thou relationships and a communal identity that overcomes tribal differences and grievances to achieve greater social justice for all.

Chapter 7

Deep Ecology

The prosperity and abundance many of us enjoy have led to an explosion of knowledge, capability, and creativity. But there has been a profound cost. The environment of the planet is in peril. A looming mass extinction, the overfishing and "plastification" of our oceans, and the catastrophic consequences of climate change demonstrate how humanity is altering the basic, life-giving systems on the planet and, in the process, imperiling ourselves and countless other living things.

Even though there are now millions of groups and organizations that are aware and taking action on all aspects of the various crises, the general response of individuals and institutions has been to continue the path toward unsustainability. Some are now advocating a radical change in our assumptions about the inherent value of perpetual economic growth.[1]

Most of the major institutions and governments in the world lack both passion and a sense of duty to serve and preserve the integrity of our biosphere. We belong to nature. We are

---

[1] For example, the Pachamama Alliance is an international nonprofit effort to demonstrate the connectivity of environmental sustainability, social justice, and spiritual fulfillment, with the goal of motivating individuals and communities to act. The Pachamama Alliance argues that if the industrial North reduced its consumption of natural resources, it would reduce the pressure on the rainforest, the home of native people in Central and South America.

dependent on nature. Further alienation from nature will be at our own peril.[2]

In nature, when there is a disturbance (for example, fire, drought, disease, infestations), there is an intermediate state before recovery. The disturbance is necessary for the new to emerge. In between there is a liminal state, a bedrock of possibilities in which the system stops and surrenders. When a tree is injured, pheromones are sent out to other trees through their entangled roots.

Michael Kalten, a professor of religion at the University of Washington, proposes a "green spirituality," a spirituality of horizontal transcendence. Rather than assume matter is lifeless, a green spirituality sees matter as the source of all the rich and varied phenomena of life and consciousness. Kalten writes: "Reductionist science . . . has insistently explained the vitality of our bodies and minds in terms of chemical and complex electric functions that presumably have no vitality [in and of themselves]." The wholeness model and the holistic approach advocated by Kalten suggests differently. "Matter is alive when it is at the complex level of metabolic and self-reproduction processes," but also at less complex levels. In "a living Universe . . . all life is understood as a phenomenon just waiting for the right level of complexity to appear."[3]

Major Barriers to Deep Relationships to Nature

The new creation story of an emergent universe describes how connected we are to all living things. We were not added to the earth by a divine being after the earth was created. We came out of the earth, which formed out of space debris and stardust. Brian Swimme writes, "The planet Earth, once molten rock, now

---

[2] Espen Hammer, "A Utopia for a Dystopian Age," *New York Times*, June 25, 2017.

[3] Michael Kalten, "Green Spirituality: Horizontal Transcendence," in *The Psychology of Mature Spirituality: Integrity, Wisdom, Transcendence*, ed. Polly Young-Eisendrath and Melvin E. Miller (Philadelphia: Taylor and Francis, 2000), 198.

sings opera."[4] Some ancient creation stories also honor our origin from the earth. Jewish theology claims that the first human is *ha'adam*, which means "the ground." God took "the ground," and God made, formed, then breathed life into it.

Theologians build on the new universe story by asserting that wisdom was present from the beginning. Most believe that

> a Creator Spirit dwells at the heart of the natural world, graciously energizing its evolution from within, compassionately holding all creatures in their finitude and death, and drawing the world forward toward an unimaginable future. Through the vast sweep of cosmic and biological evolution, the Spirit embraces the material root of life and its endless new potential, empowering the cosmic process from within. The universe, in turn, is self-organizing and self-transcending, energized from the spiraling galaxies to the double helix of the DNA molecule by the dance of divine vivifying power.[5]

Jungian analyst Jerome Bernstein provides a fascinating account of the development of the Western ego from a historical interpretation of the Bible to our present disconnect from the natural world. Bernstein believes that this development has moved the Western psyche away from its roots in nature into an ever more abstracted intellectual consciousness. He also sees an evolutionary shift in psychic consciousness that brings a growing number of individuals into contact with nature.[6]

Bernstein uses the term *transrational reality* to describe the nonpersonal, nonrational phenomena occurring in the natural universe. The transrational reality is not explainable by our standard cause-and-effect logical structures. There is also a cultural

---

[4] Brian Swimme, *The Hidden Heart of the Cosmos: Humanity and the New Story* (Maryknoll, NY: Orbis Books, 1999).

[5] Elizabeth Johnson, *Quest for the Living God: Mapping Frontiers in the Theology of God* (New York: Continuum, 2007), 191.

[6] Jerome Bernstein, *Living in the Borderland: The Evolution of Consciousness and the Challenge of Healing Trauma* (New York: Routledge, 2005).

and psychological bias against transrational experiences, such as dreams. Bernstein says the transrational experience is a sacred mystery connected to the source of life itself, a dimension that preexisted before any concept of a personified deity. This is the essence of the core in the wholeness model.

To move from the abstract intellectual constructs and claims to superior and absolute knowledge through science that suppresses knowledge about transrational reality, we must go to the bedrock and our deep connection with nature.

Bernstein provides stories of individuals who are experiencing this evolutionary shift of consciousness to transrational reality and sensitivity to all things animate and inanimate. He argues passionately for a new paradigm for the healing of trauma through a reconnecting of the Western medical model with a body-mind-spirit approach, most notably that of the Navajo medical model:

> We must also reassess our most basic concepts of what we consider normal and what we consider pathological. And it would behoove us to consider that labeling a feeling or a behavior as pathological might sometimes be our defense against having to recognize that we live in a dissociated culture, one that reacts in terror of recognizing that we are not all powerful and that human life is dependent on its relationship to all life.[7]

Transrational people are reorienting their ego-driven life to a life that quests for wholeness. R. D. Laing states:

> What we call "normal" is a product of repression, denial, splitting, projection, introjection, and other forms of destructive action on experience. . . . The "normally" alienated person, by reason of the fact that he acts more or less like everyone else, is taken to be sane. . . . The condition of alienation . . . of being unconscious . . . is the condition of normal man. Society highly values its normal man. It

---

[7] Jerome S. Bernstein, "Living in the Borderland: Healing the Split between Psyche and Nature," Psyche and Nature Conference, Santa Barbara, California, March 2007.

educates children to lose themselves and to become absurd, and thus to be normal.[8]

What Do We Really Need?

Much of modern life involves shopping for essentials like food and clothing. But we also shop for things we don't need but that we desire. Why is this?

While working on this chapter, I had this dream:

> My wife and I are looking at the items for sale in a large home. The prices are not clear. The items are mostly small and Asian. There is a chess set, small bowls, salt and pepper shakers. The owner is there. We pull out drawer after drawer and see amazing things. Some that we want had already been sold. Others cost one dollar, but we are not clear which ones we can buy. Some are cheap, some expensive.

The dream raises the question of what I really need. I am attracted to many objects, many "shiny objects," but often I am not clear that I need them or that they are even available to me.

In the dream I search for what I can have. I clearly need to sort out what is obtainable and what is valuable. I am reminded of the parable of the pearl of great price and my need to discern what is most important. Many of the objects in the dream, although desirable, could become idols. Sanguin writes:

> Every doctrine that has lost its original aliveness and context becomes an idol. Every piece of music which is merely trendy and imitative is idolatrous. Our very thinking process is an idol when it simply defaults to dead and lifeless stories, but doesn't participate in the vibrancy and spontaneity of this moment. Scripture becomes an idol and the study of it idolatrous when it is taken either literally by fundamentalists, or is deconstructed and disconnected from

---

[8] R. D. Laing, *The Politics of Experience/The Bird of Paradise* (New York: Pantheon Books, 1983), 27–28.

its numinous source by biblical scholars. The self is in constant danger of being exploited as an idol by a world that is increasingly reducing the human to a consumer. . . . When we can no longer feel that we are being lived by the Whole, by the Originating Mystery, and that every experience is an invitation to respond spontaneously to this presence that is living us, we are in danger of becoming idols and idolaters.[9]

Only by connecting to the bedrock, the "Originating Mystery" that Sanguin refers to, can I avoid making an idol of most things on the surface.

The story of Jesus and his apostles fishing helps to make this point. The apostles were continually casting their nets on the left side of the boat. They were caught up in a habitual pattern that was not yielding any results. When Jesus said to cast the nets over the right side of the boat, their nets were filled. As an analogy, it suggests there is abundance in our unconscious (the bedrock), but we are limited by our patterns. In terms of the cycle of becoming model, we sometimes only venture to the middle, where we find emotions that reinforce our *desires*. By casting our net to the bedrock, we find what we really *need*, the love and wholeness we long for.

Attachment and Addiction

The challenge is to shift from desire to longing. Desire is never satisfied. It is the smaller constricted self that is prone to addictions. Our longing is not meant to be satisfied. Our longing continually propels us to the bedrock to find inner freedom, the ability to let go. Without freedom from our attachments on the surface, we cannot love fully and unconditionally.

Our egos tie us to the attachments of things, people, times and places, reputation and image, professions, our ideas, success, and to life itself. Clinging to money and possessions can enslave us. We should enjoy life and the pleasure it brings. The problem is

---

[9] Bruce Sanguin, "Owen Barfield Rocks: Part Two—Idols and Idolatry," blog.

our selfish inability to let go of these things when we are challenged by the needs of others.

Jesus's radical freedom is that he was able to give all of this up freely. By freeing ourselves from attachments and habits and "casting our nets" into the bedrock, we can begin to experience this same freedom.

The bedrock of possibilities has everything and does not require any particular thing. The love and wisdom we find there are not attachments. They are our essential being; they provide the freedom to disengage from harmful attachments on the surface.

Arthur Brooks suggests three practices to avoid attachment on the surface.

> First, collect experiences, not things. . . . It is the physically permanent stuff that evaporates from our minds. It is memories in the ether of our consciousness that last a lifetime, there for us to enjoy again and again.
>
> Second, steer clear of . . . a dogged pursuit of practicality and usefulness at all costs. For those of us blessed to be above poverty . . . excessive focus on your finances obscures what you are supposed to enjoy with them.
>
> Finally, make sure you know what is the transcendental truth at the center of your wheel, and make that your focus.[10]

Brooks's "transcendental truth at the center" is the bedrock in the wholeness model. His advice is especially important in detaching from the contemporary technologies that have become addictive.

Sacredness of the Earth

Deep ecology is a philosophy of nature that sees the environmental crisis as a symptom of a psychological or spiritual ailment afflicting modern humanity. This philosophy holds that humans have an illusion of separation from

---

[10] Arthur Brooks, "Abundance without Attachment," *New York Times*, December 14, 2014, 1, 4.

nature, by anthropocentrism or human centeredness. Deep ecology critiques the idea that we are the crown of creation, the measure of all being: that the world is a pyramid with humanity rightly on top, merely a resource, and that nature has instrumental value only.[11]

The term *deep ecology* was coined in the 1970s by Arne Naess, professor emeritus of philosophy at Oslo University. He and other deep ecology theorists have traced the historical roots of anthropocentrism to the belief that only humans were created in the image of God, only humans have a soul, and prophetically, humans have dominion over all living things.[12]

A powerful image of God is breath, the life force of earth: plants breathing out oxygen for animals to breathe in; animals breathing out carbon dioxide for plants to take in. If we think about breath in this moment of human and planetary crisis, we can see deep ecology as the intention to participate in God's creative, generative breath.

To do the work of transformation, we need to listen deeply to the wisdom of the natural order, art, music, and science and realize we are not at the center of creation.

The will to help with our ecological crises—climate change, eradication of plant and animal species, deforestation, ocean pollution, and environmental refugees—will come once we realize how deeply our existence depends on the planet with which we share life.

We usually think of relationship as something occurring between two people. But when we are in relationship with a person, we are also in a relationship with everything in the world that affects that relationship.

Fishes think and feel. HOW do we know that being petted feels good to a fish? They ask for it. Friendly groupers swim up to divers to receive strokes, and moray eels will cuddle with trusted divers. Even some shark species love

---

[11] John Seed, "The Ecological Self," *EarthLight Magazine #53*, vol. 14, no. 4 (Spring 2005).

[12] Arne Naess, *The Ecology of Wisdom: Writings by Arne Naess*, ed. Alan Drengson and Bill Devail (Berkeley, CA: Counterpoint, 2010).

getting face and belly rubs from experienced divers (don't try this yourself).[13]

Francis Rothluebber says that to become a co-creator with God we need to awaken to these amazing relationships. It requires "coming closer and closer until there is a fusing, a living in Oneness, inter-abiding, a living exchange of life lovingly."[14]

Among those concerned about our ecology there is general agreement that the world is sacred. The success of the movie *Avatar* is an indication that many support finding ways to preserve the planet and all forms of life.

Keystone species are those that have a disproportionate effect relative to their abundance. If a keystone species is removed from the environment, there is a sharp decline in diversity, many other species become extinct, and one species takes over. A keystone consumer is a small group that can precipitate the disappearance of an entire species, for example, seafood lovers whose over-consumption wipes out a species. We need to protect keystone species and curb keystone consumption.

When we realize that human beings are on a continuum of incarnation with stars, the solar system, earth, minerals, plants, and animals—the latest or most recent form of emergence—we understand what our indigenous people intuited: we are kin with all creation. This is a fundamental reorientation and correction of the modernist mindset. It is a reclaiming of lost wisdom that truly enables us to honor earth and not simply exploit earth as a resource to be consumed.

Given such deep roots in culture and psyche, it is little wonder that a change of concepts by itself is not sufficient to reorient and align us back with the flow. As Naess points out, ecological ideas are not enough; we need an ecological identity, an ecological self. Ideas engage only one part of our brain, the frontal lobe, and cognition. We need ecological feelings and actions as well as ideas to nurture ecological identity. Henry

---

[13] Jonathan Balcombe, "Fishes Have Feelings Too," *New York Times*, May 15, 2016, SR9.

[14] Francis Rothluebber, *Who Creates the Future: Discovering the Essential Energy of Co-Creation* (Idyllwild, CA: Womenspace, 2016), 36.

David Thoreau challenged human insensitivity to the suffering of "mere" animals:

> Salmon, shad, and alewives were formerly abundant here, and taken in weirs by the Indians . . . until the dam and afterward the canal at Billerica, and the factories at Lowell, put an end to their migrations hitherward. . . . Armed with no sword, no electric shock, but mere Shad, armed only with innocence and a just cause. . . . I for one am with thee, and who knows what may avail a crow-bar against that Billerica dam? Away with the superficial and selfish philanthropy of men,—who knows what admirable virtue of fishes may be below low water-mark, bearing up against a hard destiny, not admired by the fellow creature who alone can appreciate it! Who hears the fishes when they cry?[15]

Thoreau mourns the fate of the shad when the Billerica Dam was built. Are we aware of our environmental impact? Who hears the fishes when they cry?

This age of ecological devastation of earth is a reenactment of crucifixion. Stories of the comeback of species, of the reclamation of watersheds, of rivers that are flowing clean again, of reconstituted soil, of human beings living more simply that others may simply live, of a human being who awakens to the gift of her own body—these are the new Easter stories. They speak, for those with ears to hear, of a primordial and unceasing sacred impulse to heal, to restore, and to rise out of death.

> Unless we find a way to regularly practice our deep ecology, the new and fragile consciousness fades back into the logic of the eddy and we remain trapped inside a skin encapsulated ego floating helplessly towards the abyss. The ideas of interconnectedness and participation may remain, but in the absence of the experience they are sterile. These things are best explored in community. We need to find . . . opportunities to meet—on solstices, equinoxes, under

---

[15] Henry David Thoreau, *A Week on the Concord and Merrimack Rivers* (Princeton, NJ: Princeton University Press, 2004 <1849>).

the full moon, in deep ecology workshops, or on-line to build these vital support systems into our lives. In such ways, whilst swirling in the midst of the vast eddy, we may remain aligned to the flow.[16]

Surrendering our fears makes room inside our heads and lives for the arrival of unexpected grace, the presence of the sacred from the bedrock. We then are free to go with the flow.

Recognizing Loss

Because of our separation from other species, we usually don't experience loss when they go extinct or even when they lose the environment and land they depend on. To experience loss, we need to feel the common stakes we have in our mutual existence. We need the imaginative power in the bedrock to trigger the feelings of loss.

Following is an example of loss I have experienced, not at the time the loss happened, but later in life when I realized how my early joy was linked to what I have lost.

During my junior and senior high school years, I lived with my parents on a farm near Jackson, Minnesota. On the eighty-acre farm was a winding creek with interesting shallow and deep pools where in the spring I saw fish, especially as they swam over the shallows. It was a tranquil place, part of a pasture where our cows could come to drink. I spent many pleasant hours throughout the summer fascinated by the twists and turns of the creek and the ebb and flow of the water and the fish. Upon graduation, I went away to college. Several years later when I visited the farm I saw that the creek had been replaced by a large straight ditch that enabled my father to cultivate more acreage for crops. I didn't think much about it at the time, being preoccupied with college and my girlfriend (future wife) who I had brought to meet my parents.

---

[16] Seed, "The Ecological Self.

It was only much later in life that I realized the loss to myself and to the fish and wildlife that loved that creek. My time at the creek was sacred. The loss I continue to feel moves me emotionally and in my bedrock of meaning.

The loss of the creek continues to generate emotions in me that force my awareness of the sacredness of nature and the limits to which we humans should go. We can't uncouple from nature. Believing that we are smart and creative enough to improve on nature is foolish; it is even a crime against nature. We need to live within our limits.

On a recent trip to the farm I saw that the farm buildings, including the house, were gone. The only thing remaining was a single shed used for storing some farm implements for the corporation that now owns the farm and many other farms in the county. No one lived there, but the grove of trees remained. The grove stood like a sentinel of a former life and time when my family and animals sought shade there. As I drove around the county, I saw that the same pattern was repeated—groves of trees on sections of farm land with no humans living there. It was sad to see this, yet hopeful. I had recently read about sacred groves. In urban areas they are essential for maintaining social capital at the sacred-urban nexus.[17] The interdependent exchange between the essential grove and urban life could be considered as an archetype of paradise.

Groves on the vanishing homesteads in the Midwest could be considered sacred sentinels. The modernist worldview, which objectifies the natural world as little more than nonsentient resources for human consumption, is leading us to a point of no return. What is urgently required is to regain a felt connection to the natural world as intelligent, sentient, and inherently worthy of flourishing. The owners of the vast sections of land may unconsciously realize this. Otherwise, why not chop down the groves for lumber? We are not truly conscious of how inextricably embedded we are in nature. We are nature in the form

---

[17] David Grace, "Seeing the Sacred Grove from the Trees: Uncovering Social Capital at the Sacred-Urban Nexus," paper presented at the International Society for the Study of Religion, Nature, and Culture, Gainesville, Florida, University of Florida, June 14–17, 2016.

of humans. There is no separation. Our task now is not to rule over nature, even as stewards, but to take our place in grace.

Our fantasies, anxieties and defenses are expressed in these three statements:

1. It's not happening.
2. It's not my fault.
3. There is nothing we can do about it (so I can get on with my life as usual).[18]

An old Ojibway man was asked, "Are rocks alive?"
He replied, "Some are."
He was referring to specific rocks in specific places. For native peoples, specific rocks and objects in nature are treated differently as objects. Winona LaDuke says that a stone is an animate noun. For example, she says the twenty-five-hundred-pound copper boulder at the Smithsonian is an old being that needs to be returned to its place.[19]

This deep sense of place seems to be increasingly fragmented in the modern world. Technology allows us to occupy more than one place, space, and community simultaneously. We have more places where we can experience meaning and find community, but we can also seem distant from the place we are really "in" at the moment.

The practices of deep ecology, calming our minds and going to the bedrock can increase our ability to be fully aware of the beauty and interrelationships of the place we are in the moment and commune more deeply with the world as it is.

The question to the old man should have been, "With what rocks do you have a relationship?"

To avoid loss we need to ask: "What do I relate to?" "To what am I responsive?" "What transforms me?" Answering "What

---

[18] Joseph Dodds, *Psychoanalysis and Ecology at the Edge of Chaos: Complexity Theory, Deleuze, Guattari, and Psychoanalysis for a Climate in Crisis* (New York: Routledge, 2011), 43.

[19] Winona LaDuke, lecture at the International Society for the Study of Religion, Nature, and Culture, Gainesville, Florida, University of Florida, June 14–17, 2016.

do I eat?" provides important facts about your relationship to animals and plants. For what or whom do you care? We are members of a multispecies, multilayered environment. We have a collective responsibility for the well-being of everything in a given place, for the wholeness of it all, especially if the members cannot protect themselves, like the dodo bird.[20]

The wild natural places around us are repositories of personal memories of our encounters and experiences with the intimacy of nature that helped shape our understanding of what it means to be human.

> To walk into such places daily is to be delivered into the possibility of escape—from ourselves, our fears and worries and the increasing madness of this human world. To do so reminds us that we are part of a greater and more beautiful planet than we often take the time to remember. And right now we need that as surely as we need anything.[21]

A wild place in nature, like a spring bubbling up from the earth, is valuable for us humans, but it also has value in itself.

> Its life-giving character is an aspect of its intrinsic power, a power that is present whether or not human beings are sustained by it. The spring does not achieve value merely through human agency, as an anthropocentric perspective might claim. Rather, its mere existence as a member of the community of Earth is the basis of its value. Its ability to sustain and nurture life flows from this and exemplifies the interconnectedness of Earth's living creatures as well as human beings' complete dependence on it.[22]

---

[20] Dodo birds vanished so quickly from the island of Mauritius because they had no natural predators and thus no need to evolve any natural defenses. Dodo birds were so innately trusting that they would actually waddle up to armed Dutch settlers, unaware that these strange creatures intended to kill and eat them.

[21] Rob Cowen, "Where Nature Gets to Run Amok," *New York Times*, April 16, 2017, SR8.

[22] Diane Bergant, *A New Heaven, a New Earth: The Bible and Catholicity* (Maryknoll, NY: Orbis Books, 2016), 25.

We respect nature when we realize the intrinsic value of the wild places, when we realize natural phenomena have the right to exist and need to be preserved. When we tamper with or destroy those wild places, we are affecting places that are life-giving for us and for others.

We respect our environment when we demonstrate gratitude, relate constructively to others, and limit our use to what is needed so that others may flourish.

Our relationships constitute our self. At our core is no-self. We are internally related to the integrated social and natural environments. We are super-ecosystems—we contain many species of microbial symbionts from the top all the way down, for example, those necessary for digestion. We are more microbial than human. "Even when we are alone, we are never alone."[23]

Practical Steps

We do not need to fix everything ourselves—we cannot! But each one of us can take on a moral issue and fight at least one battle, for example, habitat degradation, ozone depletion, loss of forests, loss of arable land, dead zones at river mouths, toxic environments, melting glaciers, mass extinction of large animals. We cannot control all the factors causing these crises, such as increased population. On the other hand, we must not succumb to a sense of being overwhelmed.

Spiritual transformation is more likely to occur when we act into belief rather than when we try to believe into action. How we live what we say is more relevant and important than what we say.

Some ways to participate in deep ecology include the following:

- Reconsider any stereotypes we have about environmentalists.
- Some religious ideologies limit our caring for the planet; explore alternatives ones that embrace wholeness.

---

[23] Ed Yong, *I Contain Multitudes: The Microbes within Us and a Grander View of Life* (New York: HarperCollins, 2016), 3.

- Identify the choices that perpetuate global warming and make new choices that will generate different outcomes.
- Take personal responsibility. Do we assign blame only to Big Oil, Wall Street, and so on?
- Discuss the views of scientists, particularly those who model climate change.
- Look beyond our materialistic culture. Are we imposing our beliefs about use of natural resources on others who share this planet?
- Listen to other views and dialogue to understand the issues.

Conclusion

Joanna Macy coined the term *The Great Turning* as the transition from an industrial growth society to a life-sustaining society with three simultaneous and mutually reinforcing dimensions:

- Holding Actions—frontline, direct actions to stop or limit the immediate damage as well as all political, legal, and legislative work.
- Life-sustaining Systems—solutions that address structural causes of the crises and offer alternative models.
- Shift in Consciousness—a profound shift in our perception of reality, our values, our attitudes, our goals.[24]

Macy cautions that there is no guarantee that we will make this transition in time for the survival of civilization or evolution of complex life systems. Yet, it is the hope that it is not too late that should spur us to find our passion to act, which will inform and sustain us in striving to bring forth the Great Turning.

---

[24] Joanna Macy and Chris Johnstone, *Active Hope: How to Face the Mess We're In without Going Crazy* (New World Library, 2012), 27–31.

Wild Mercy

The eyes of the future are looking back at us and they are praying for us to see beyond our time. They are kneeling with clasped hands hoping that we might act with restraint, that we might leave room for the life that is destined to come. To protect what is wild is to protect what is gentle. Perhaps the wildness we fear is the pause between our own heartbeats, the silence that reminds us we live only by grace.[25]

Wild mercy is in our hands.

---

[25] Terry Tempest Williams, "Op-Ed: Wild Mercy," newsroom/op-ed, http://www.hifrontier.com/libtree/News/tempest.html. See also idem, *Refuge: An Unnatural History of Family and Place* (New York: Vintage, 1991).

Chapter 8

Deep Moral Agency

> *Act always as if the future of the universe depended on what you did, while laughing at yourself for thinking that whatever you do makes any difference. (Buddhist proverb)*

> *We have different gifts, according to the grace given to each of us. If your gift is prophesying, then prophesy in accordance with your faith; if it is serving, then serve; if it is teaching, then teach; if it is to encourage, then give encouragement; if it is giving, then give generously; if it is to lead, do it diligently; if it is to show mercy, do it cheerfully. (Romans 12:6–8, The Message)*

I chose the word *agency* for the title of this chapter. *Agency* is the capacity to act and exert power. Other terms could have been *leading, teaching, creating, exploring, imagining,* or *risking.* *Moral agency* is "an individual's ability to make choices based on some common standard of right and wrong and to be held accountable for these actions."[1]

We are all moral role models for someone. Daily we influence those around us. We affect the lives of others so we can mutually benefit from being together.

On February 6, I had this dream:

> I am a consultant to a business executive. A woman is with me. She briefly talks about the importance of feedback. I then ask the executive, "Would you like some feedback?" He agrees. I tell him that I know why he is such a successful negotiator. I tell him that when I asked him a question, he replied with substance and content but forcefully. I say that I was not able to respond because he just overwhelmed me about the topic. I had nothing else to say. After hearing this observation, his demeanor softened. He showed me around his place. I was missing a musical instrument. We looked, in case it was there.

My reflection on the dream: My feedback was not an attack on the executive but rather an "I" statement about his impact on me. I told him that his manner of arguing had shut me down. In the dream this apparently disarmed him and he softened his approach and accepted me, even including and supporting me on my quest for something I had lost.

I believe the dream is about being a moral agent—the focus of this chapter. To be a moral presence in the face of power or opposition, the correct stance is nonviolent resistance. Like the approach of Gandhi and Martin Luther King, Jr., the challenge is to show the dominant powers the impact they are having on others. By helping them to realize that their behavior is devastating to others, their inner bedrock of grace and love is stirred. They realize that this is not the outcome they want.

As we apply the wholeness and cycle of becoming models to the topics we have explored—self-development, relationships, and ecology—the process is not likely to be neat and orderly. There will be ambiguity, contradictions, hesitation, and moments

---

[1] Angus Taylor, *Animals and Ethics: An Overview of the Philosophical Debate* (Peterborough, Ontario: Broadview Press, 2003), 17.

when we wonder if anything we do makes a difference. This chapter is intended to provide encouragement that something creative will emerge out of these moments of uncertainty. When we engage the bedrock of body, mind, and soul, we are connected to powerful, mysterious forces. Margaret Wheatley reminds us that the activity of leading is "spiritual work":

> Leaders seek realignment with our internal guidance, our spiritual self. It is with this greater mindfulness of one another and of our interconnectedness with our Earth and One Another that new and enlightened leaders will remember, again and again, who they are, powerful co-creators reaching out together for a more joyful, more abundant and more equitable world for everyone.
>
> It is spiritual work because leaders deal with the cyclical nature of things, meanings that motivate service, courage, and interconnections with all life.[2]

Moral agency is about stretching our imagination, encouraging novelty, facing the uncertainties, and taking risks about when and where to influence our surroundings.

Being a Moral Leader

Effective moral leaders lead from their life experience. They share their life with others. They are not like the preacher described by Ralph Waldo Emerson:

> I once heard a preacher who sorely tempted me to say, I would go to church no more. . . . If he had ever lived and acted, we were none the wiser for it. The capital secret of his profession, namely, to convert life into truth, he had not learned. Not one fact in all his experience, had he yet imported into his doctrine. This man had ploughed, and planted, and talked, and bought, and sold; he had read books; he had eaten and drunken; his head aches; his heart

---

[2] Margaret Wheatley, *Finding Our Way: Leadership for an Uncertain Time* (San Francisco: Berrett-Koehler, 2007), 126.

throbs; he smiles and suffers; yet was there not a surmise, a hint, in all the discourse, that he had ever lived at all. Not a line did he draw out of real history. The true preacher can be known by this, that he deals out to the people his life,—life passed through the fire of thought.[3]

Leaders who have accessed the deep wisdom of the bedrock and relate it to their life experiences are best able to offer spiritual insights and avoid providing false certainty and telling others what to think.

By sharing their own narrative of resiliency based on their life experience, moral agents can develop relationships that create more space for others to speak their fears and uncertainties and bring what they are passionate about to the surface.

These relationships help others to find their purpose in life and to feel useful. As a personal example, I have participated in a major mission of my church, Feed the 5,000, at Thanksgiving. The program is immensely successful because of the obvious outcome—the gratitude of those receiving the meals. But less obvious is what it does for the hundred volunteers who prepare for the day, cook the turkeys, and deliver the meals to the homes of persons in need. The volunteers feel needed!

Be Disruptive

To help living systems stay healthy and evolve, at times a moral agent needs to be disruptive of an oppressive status quo, hero-ically standing for the truth revealed in the bedrock in the face of a disbelieving world. When we manifest the moral courage to step forward, take responsibility for what is happening, and become exemplars of what is possible, we can make a significant difference in the world. Some examples of disruption:

- Rosa Parks refused to surrender her seat.
- Civil rights activists marched across the Edmund Pettus Bridge.

---

[3] Ralph Waldo Emerson, address to Divinity College, Cambridge, July 15, 1838.

- Wikileaks—whether you love it or hate it.
- Uber.
- Bitcoin.
- LGBT people fought back at the Stonewall Inn.

Many forms of disruption require going to the bedrock for courage and support. It is helpful to also have friends and allies, but often it is the courage of one who takes a stand that starts a movement.

The resistance to change is based on fear of a perceived threat. To meet this resistance without becoming as oppressive as the status quo, it is vital to engage the resistance in each of the strata of the wholeness model.

At the surface a moral agent needs to interpret events and help clarify what is happening. At the middle stratum the agent needs to identify emotions and clarify motivations. At the bedrock a moral agent needs to name the mysteries, including the universal longing for compassion. Done patiently and without ego, acceptance of novel resolutions becomes more possible. This is creative leadership of the many, a leadership of hope.

When we are connected to the bedrock we bring forth a future that is grounded in love and wisdom. We reflect God's light and love outward to creation where it can be reflected to us. We become conscious of new options for action.

According to John Beebe, the integrity of moral leaders depends upon claiming the "spine" of their personality, both embracing the strengths and accepting the shadow, the blind spot. This is the inner basis of the uprightness we look for in ourselves and in each other.[4] When we cycle to the bedrock, we encounter our blind spots, but we also gain insights into the whole of life. When we are sensitive to the needs of the whole, we have integrity and a deep relationship with others.

Leaders with integrity have tapped into the wisdom of the bedrock and experienced their own spiritual authority. They have accepted the challenges to be servants of the whole.

Peter Senge and his colleagues, acting from a connection to the bedrock, popularized the idea of *presence,* an awareness

---

[4] John Beebe, *Integrity in Depth* (College Station: Texas A&M University Press, 1992).

of the larger whole, leading to actions that can help to shape its evolution and our future.[5] In their discussion, recorded in their book *Presence,* they frame the whole that a leader serves as follows:

> What we're talking about is sensing the unfolding whole within each of us, within the present situation, and acting in service of it. . . . The other notion of whole, the "integrated global agenda" notion of whole, is what leads to the dead end that [physicist and philosopher of science Henri] Bortoft calls "the counterfeit whole." . . . Another paradox. Serving the emerging whole means paying attention to what's right here within my awareness, what's completely local, and surrendering to what's being asked of me now. . . .
>
> The deepest systems we enact are woven into the fabric of everyday life, down to the most minute detail. This is so important for us to understand. We, every one of us, may be able to change the world, but only as we experience more and more of the whole in the present. This is the "evolving consciousness" that [physicist David] Bohm said was necessary to appreciate the implicate order. . . . [It's] also the cultivation of awareness to "see the absolute in the manifest," as the Buddhists would say." And only as we learn to use ourselves as instruments for something larger than ourselves to emerge, wherever we act . . . as parents or citizens or community organizers or managers in global corporations. . . .
>
> There's no other way out of this. We may not be able to change the larger systems overnight, but we can commit to the continual development of awareness and the capacity to choose. . . .
>
> The core of presencing is waking up together—waking up to who we really are by linking with and acting from our highest future Self—and by using the Self as a vehicle

---

[5] Peter M. Senge, C. Otto Scharmer, Joseph Jaworski, and Betty Sue Flowers, *Presence: An Exploration of Profound Change in People, Organizations, and Society* (New York: Crown Publishing Group, 2004), 228–32,

for bringing forth new worlds . . . it's the point where the fire of creation burns and enters the world through us.[6]

Moral Agency in the Work Place

An essential aspect of moral agency is the capacity to love, which was presented in Part I. Our culture does not speak of or nurture this kind of love in our work places, but we need to change that to bring the bedrock and core to bear in this major aspect of human life. Deep moral agency in a work place requires people working collectively to ask themselves what they are about, what they need, and where their insights are leading them.

For employees to receive altruistic love, managers need to create the conditions that foster hope and faith in the organization's purpose. A socially responsible vision is a great motivator. Motivated, respected, and loved employees provide socially responsible service to customers and other organization stakeholders.[7]

For many managers I have worked with, being a moral agent is a vocation that gives their life purpose and meaning. They demonstrate care for their colleagues by providing positive feedback and appreciation. They also continually reevaluate the impact their policies and procedures have on the organization's culture.

Regarding moral leadership in secular organizations, Charles Handy, a former executive of Shell Oil and professor at the London Business School, says that meditation, prayer, and mental and physical exercises aid self-responsibility and the strength to persevere.[8]

Holistic leaders strive to help individuals find meaning in their work. Genuine concern for the whole person is reflected in questions such as: Who are we as a work team? Is our work worthy? What is our greater purpose? What are our values and ethical

---

[6] Ibid., 214–15, 238, 240.

[7] L. W. Fry, "The Spiritual Leadership Balanced Scorecard Business Model: The Case of the Cordon Bleu-Tomasso Corporation," *Journal of Management, Spirituality, and Religion* 7, no. 4 (2010): 283–314.

[8] Charles Handy, *The Hungry Spirit: Beyond Capitalism: A Quest for Purpose in the Modern World* (New York: Broadway Books), 1998.

principles? What will be our legacy? A spiritual leader strives for a work place that is a genuine community, consisting of people with shared traditions, values, and beliefs, and focused on transformation, diversity, partnership, collaboration, and inspiration.

As organizations reassess their purpose by going deep into the collective bedrock, they tap into a power higher than a profit motive. The transformation needs to be at all levels in the organization—individually in the leaders and the employees, but also in the policies and procedures, use of corporate assets, fair dealings with stakeholders, and reporting illegal or unethical behaviors.

Manish Chopra, a principal in McKinsey's New York office and author of *The Equanimous Mind*, provides a good example of how meditation has helped him to deal with three common challenges faced by leaders: email addiction, coping with disappointment, and becoming too insular.

> Through meditation, my self-awareness and self-regulation "muscles" have grown to the point where I now am better able, after a good night's rest, to put the first several hours of my day to better use: toward meditating, exercising, writing, planning the day's priorities, and other complex-thinking tasks that would likely be crowded out later. . . .
>
> Although meditation is a solitary act, it has helped me focus more on others as I shed some of my insecurities and redefined the way I make tough trade-offs. I used to feel insecure about being "left out" of certain meetings or discussions, thereby passing up opportunities to delegate. Similarly, when I faced dilemmas that required balancing conflicting interests, my dominant consideration was "What's in it for me?" . . .
>
> What's also shifted is my definition of personal gain or loss. I still acknowledge the personal dimension, but I find myself slowing down, and reflecting on situations from more angles, including more of how the situation will affect other people or the environment in which we live, and of what's right or fair. The impact of a decision on me personally is less of a yoke that makes the labor of assessing my choices exhausting or draining. . . .
>
> I would sum up my experience in four words: observe more, react less. I try to observe myself more disinterestedly

and to avoid knee-jerk reactions to the rush of incoming stimuli and to situations that seem negative. Even if I don't always succeed, I am more easily able to identify my weaknesses: my sense of insecurity, addiction to short-term benefits, and overemphasis on process-driven results. That helps me work smarter and lead better toward longer-lasting achievements.[9]

Chopra's connection to the bedrock has helped him to let go of his internal turmoil and pay attention to the external wholeness of his world.

Moral Teaching in Groups

As he has gone deeper in his spiritual practice, Christopher Bache describes how his presence in the classroom triggered a deep response from his students, a "deeply felt transmission of insight underneath a verbal exchange, the transfer of the essence of an insight or experience." His own awakening has also been influenced by the collective consciousness in what he calls "the living classroom."

> When people open themselves to each other and focus intensely on a common goal, their individual energies become synchronized . . . with levels of intelligence and creativity that are beyond the reach of these same individuals acting alone. We must engage each other in an integrated manner for this more potent mode of knowing to emerge.[10]

I also have let my experience in the bedrock trigger the collective unconscious in groups I have led. What I did with my dream in January 2016 during a week I was preparing a presentation about the soul and the quantum for my adult spiritual

---

[9] Manish Chopra, "Want to Be a Better Leader? Observe More and React Less," *McKinsey Quarterly* (February 2016).

[10] Christopher W. Bache, *The Living Classroom: Teaching and Collective Consciousness*, SUNY Series in Transpersonal and Humanistic Psychology (Albany: State University of New York Press, 2010), 68.

enrichment group is an example. The dream was this: "I am try-ing to decide whether to title a seminar session 'Communication' or 'What We Can Learn from the Birds.' A colleague in the dream advises me to not forget the birds." I woke up and thought about the way McFadden and Al-Khalili describe how European robins find their way south in the winter. The birds are prompted by the quantum bedrock to know where they are going.[11]

The next day at the presentation I talked about the entangled electrons in the brains of the robins and the fast reaction of cryptochrome in the birds' eyes and asked the audience: "Are our creative mystical intuitions and dreams made possible by quantum coherence?"

I then went on to talk about how the delicate coherence at the bedrock can leak away very quickly and be lost in the incoherent noise of its surroundings, and I discussed how we destroy our moments of spiritual coherence.

The group was moved to a deeper level as the members re-flected on the meaning for them. Several shared stories about being stirred by something deep within.

Like a play within a play, my dream is an example of how I am prompted by the bedrock. These are other examples I have used to link the bedrock of mind and soul and the model of quantum biology:

- When tree leaves capture photons from the sun, they are dependent on a delicate coherence that can be maintained for biologically relevant lengths of time within the highly organized interior of a leaf. Life bridges the two realities— the physical leaf we see and the unseen quantum bedrock. *How do we bridge the physical reality of our lives and the Spirit that is moving deep within the bedrock?*
- Jesus associated God with agents (yeast, weeds), active yet hidden, persistent, creative, self-organizing, and mysterious. Quantum biology points to an even deeper level of real-ity where the Spirit acts. *The Spirit is in the possible—the seeds, hidden treasure, birds in a shrub, the dance of elec-trons in our body.*

---

[11] Johnjoe McFadden and Jim Al-Khalili, *Life on the Edge: The Com-ing of Age of Quantum Biology* (New York: Crown Publishers, 2014).

- Saint Paul wrote: "I am with you in spirit." A single atom, electron, or photon behaves like a wave that is in many places at the same time. The many electron clouds of possibility could be the "superposition" that Saint Paul intuits. When we pray for someone in a hospital, could this be a demonstration of something happening "over here" that has an instantaneous effect "over there," no matter how far away "there" is? *With deep meditation and prayer, is it possible that we can enter a coherent state where large numbers of particles in our soul are cooperating and that has effects far distant from us?*[12]

How Can We Create the Future?

How are we, as individuals, creating our future? How much agency do we have? Can even the smallest things we do contribute to developing a positive future for all sentient creatures?

James Reho quotes Saint Seraphim (1754–1833), a Russian monk, who said, "Seek your enlightenment and thousands around you will be saved."[13] Each small microcosm can contain the Cosmic Christ, who is all of reality. Saint Seraphim

> understood that healthful spiritual practice involves a deep engagement with the world. The nature of this engagement is that we mediate the uncreated light to the world, which is itself a mediator of that light in us. The reciprocity is ours by nature, as we are a self-conscious part of the web of life, of the New Jerusalem, of the mystical Body of Christ.[14]

Through our individual efforts to become enlightened, can we make a significant difference in what happens on the surface?

---

[12] I once met a Jungian analyst in Washington DC who chose to live close to the Russian embassy in order to meditate to influence the unconscious minds of embassy employees.

[13] James Reho, *Tantric Jesus: The Erotic Heart of Early Christianity* (Rochester, VT: Destiny Books, 2017), 27.

[14] Ibid., 326.

Mystical insights and practices, empirical knowledge, and the wisdom of our religious traditions all contribute to how we create the future. Our religious wisdom, mystical insights, and scientific inquiry all contribute to our discovery of a broader spirituality and engagement.

Jesus saw into the heart of reality and realized it manifested the kingdom of God. He saw the wholeness, the moment-by-moment catholicity that was creating possibility into being. By participating in Jesus's way of seeing, we can see ourselves as a manifestation of God and a moral agent of change.

Conclusion

Moral agency is the outcome of applying the wholeness model to social issues. Cycling through the model as we confront ambiguous, complex, and perplexing issues yields insights that cut through conventional wisdom.

The course is not easy, but we can be resilient as we discern what is sacred, the important relationships, and what is needed at the surface.

At times disrupting the status quo at the surface is necessary, but, by being anchored in the love and wisdom at the bedrock, we can be compassionate as we lead with integrity.

Applying the wholeness model in the work place and in our group associations can move others to a deeper level of meaning and purpose.

Part III

Wholeness in Religion and Society

In Part I, I presented the theories and models of the wholeness of body, mind, and soul and the cycle of becoming to provide an alternative way of knowing about the process of physical, mental, and spiritual development and transformation. I argued that it is essential to go to the bedrock of reality to find the wisdom and grace needed for both individual and collective development.

In Part II, I applied the theories and models to specific examples of transforming individuals, their relationships, our environment, and moral leadership. For transformation to occur, it is essential that there be purposeful human agency to evolve our biosphere to a positive future—a progression to higher levels of complexity and consciousness, toward the noosphere Teilhard has described.

In Part III, I discuss the implications of the catholicity of the wholeness model and cycling through the strata of reality for the future religious institutions and the integration of science and religion (Chapter 9) and for the future development of civilization (Chapter 10).

The argument I have presented is that by achieving and maintaining coherence in the dimensions of body, mind, and soul, we are capable of living a healthy, aware, spiritual, and fulfilling existence. I believe this is a compelling story, but is it realistic? Coherent wholeness is a transient phenomenon, but hopefully it is a state we can strive toward and attain with more frequency.

As an alternative to the dominant stories that are controlling our behavior, the wholeness story widens our perspective to a larger emerging story of catholicity.

Ken Baskin points out the value of "antenarratives" (alternative constructions of reality), which he calls "storied spaces."[1] The antenarrative encourages exploration of novel concepts that disrupt the status quo. Storied spaces generate alternative viewpoints that reflect the interplay between dominant narratives and antenarratives. This offers a more complex perception of reality equal to the complexity of our current rapidly changing environments.

The knowledge we gain from a new story connects to previous stories and new patterns are formed. Stories are like hidden layers in our psyche that build on one another to form novel complex patterns.

The complex issues we face demand a story that points to our past, contains truths about the here and now, and guides us into the future. Our issues are difficult to define, often have unseen dimensions and no clear boundaries, and are defined by many stakeholders, each with a unique worldview.

The wholeness story can frame an issue in a way that gives us a place to start and a way to revise our approach after we see what happens. The story doesn't require a perfect ending, only a direction to the potential of the next moment, what needs to emerge, and what is on the edge of the possible.

---

[1] Ken Baskin, "Storied Spaces: The Human Equivalent of Complex Adaptation," *ECO* 10, no. 2 (2008): 1–12.

Chapter 9

Deep Spirituality

*A new harmony: the Spirit, the earth,
and the human soul. The Spirit is doing a new thing. It is springing forth
now in our consciousness, among every
people, in every discipline, in every
walk of life. Do we see it? And shall
we serve it? A new Pentecost is stirring
in the human soul. Will we open to
this moment of grace and be led into
relationships of oneness we could never
before have imagined?*

—JOHN PHILIP NEWELL,
A NEW HARMONY

*The personal, mystical, immediate, and
intimate is emerging as the dominant
way of engaging the divine. What was
once reserved for a few saints has now
become the quest of millions around
the planet—to be able to touch, feel,
and know God for one's self.*

—DIANA BUTLER BASS,
GROUNDED

To explore the implications of the theory and practice of the wholeness model and the cycle of becoming for theology and religion, we need to look for wisdom in all the religious traditions. For example, the Bible, the Qur'an, the Vedas, and the Buddhist Sutras all must be seen in the context of history as an aspect of the revelation of the Divine, of the eternal wisdom that has been in the world since the creation four billion years ago and even in the beginning of our universe 13.8 billion years ago. Bede Griffiths writes:

> The "essential Truth" which is ultimately One, needs to be discovered. But this essential Truth cannot be put into words. It is not to be discovered by any process of dialectic. It is known in the silence, in the stillness of all the faculties, in the depth of the soul, beyond word and thought. It will come in different languages and expressions. In Hindu terms, it is the knowledge of the self, the divine Succedanea. In Buddhist terms, it is in the experience of Nirvana. In Muslim terms, it is *fana* and *baqa*—the passing away and the life of God. For the Jews, it is the knowledge of Yahweh, for a Christian it is the knowledge of the love of Christ which surpasses knowledge.[1]

The wholeness model is useful for both the apophatic and cataphatic aspects of the One that Bede says needs to be discovered. The core represents the silence, the depth beyond word and thought that theologians call the Apophatic Divinity. God is spontaneously and uniquely experienced by individuals in ways that cannot be expressed by words. Nor can words define the immense complexity of the Divine. The Apophatic Divinity transcends being, justice, and human love. All affirmations about God are incomplete, partial and limited. We can only say what God is not. God is always something more.

The surface in the wholeness model represents the Divine's manifestation in the world of creation. Theologians call this Cataphatic Divinity, which describes God as revealed in scripture

---

[1]   Bede Griffiths, *A New Vision of Reality: Western Science, Eastern Mysticism, and Christian Faith* (Springfield, IL: Templegate Publishers, 1990), 164.

and nature. From a cataphatic perspective humans can experience God's presence directly in each stratum of surface, middle, and bedrock. At the surface, God is experienced in nature, icons, architecture, writings, and so on. At the middle, our sense of the Cataphatic Divinity is created and personalized in images, dreams, and emotions. At the bedrock we develop a sense of a personal relation with God, who is love, transcendent, beyond our ability to contemplate.

The cycle of becoming model is a way of understanding how all the spiritual traditions evolved their core beliefs: Jews—the Law; Christians—Logos; Taoists—Eternal Tao; Buddhists—Emptiness; Hindus—Brahma; Sufi Muslims—personal experience of the Divine.[2] All traditions see the Divine with different assumptions and vocabularies, but all the traditions have progressed toward an ever-greater consciousness and deeper union with reality—a deep spirituality.

Implications for Humanity's Conception of God

Diana Butler Bass reminds us:

> The most significant story in the history of religion at this time is not a decline in Western religion, a rejection of religious institutions, or the growth of religious extremism; rather, it is a changed conception of God, a rebirthing of faith from the ground up.[3]

How does the wholeness model help us to consider the changing conception of God, which Diana Butler Bass says is today's most significant story in the history of religion? The model points to the creative energy of our transcendent experiences that gives rise to the numinous charge evoked by an experience of divine presence.[4]

---

[2] Richard Rohr, *Immortal Diamond: The Search for Our True Self* (San Francisco: Jossey-Bass, 2013), 137–38.

[3] Diana Butler Bass, *Grounded* (New York: HarperCollins Publishers, 2015), 16.

[4] James Hollis, *Finding Meaning in the Second Half of Life: How to Finally, Really Grow Up* (New York: Avery, 2006), 189.

The creative processes in the strata—surface, middle, and bedrock—of the three dimensions of body, mind, and soul are manifestations of what is generally called God. The dimensions and strata are symbolic expressions of cosmic truths that arise from the core.

A changing concept of God can expand our thinking and motivate and unite us.

God can be defined as the cause of the future that is unfolding or as the Love-Energy, the "consciousness-force that drives the fuse."[5]

> The whole of creation is moving, evolving, not only adding galaxies, but becoming, evolving within . . . Love-Energy has been driving the becoming, the evolution of the consciousness of the human family.[6]

In closing *Who Creates the Future*, Rothluebber quotes Teilhard: "The conclusion is always the same: Love is the most powerful and still the most unknown energy of the world."[7] Equating Love and God makes sense to me.

Meaningful Theology

With a changed concept of God, our theology needs to be reconsidered to be meaningful in our modern life. Theological answers are always provisional and must answer the new questions arising from our changing world.[8] There are many scholars working

---

[5] Francis Rothluebber, *Who Creates the Future: Discovering the Essential Energy of Co-Creation* (Idyllwild, CA: Womenspace, 2016), 99.

[6] Ibid., 99.

[7] Quoted in ibid., 109.

[8] Noreen Herzfeld, *Technology and Religion: Remaining Human in a Co-created World* (West Conshohocken, PA: Templeton Press, 2010), 75; Rebecca Ann Parker and Rita Nakashima Brock, *Saving Paradise: How Christianity Traded Love of This World for Crucifixion and Empire* (Boston: Beacon Press, 2009).

to that end. A recent book by Ken Wilber with the ambitious title *The Religion of Tomorrow* summarizes much of that work, especially integral theology.[9]

The theology that would emerge from the application of the wholeness and cycle of becoming models would be rooted in human experience, the same kind of experience known to our forebears in the faith. Our present-day experiences will help us to differentiate the aspects of creeds and codes that are rooted in previous cultures and traditions from the kinds of experience we share with spiritual exemplars throughout history.

Bass and Newell believe that the theology of the future will emerge from deep within the mystery of our being, all human beings, our collective unconscious, and the deep wisdom of our religious traditions (bedrock).[10] "The language of mysticism and spiritual experience . . . presents an alternative theology, that of connection and intimacy."[11]

The emergence of a new theology will be from individual and collective journeys into the forgotten and unknown depths of our souls and traditions (bedrock) and outward journeys (surface) into new ways of seeing.

In discussing the emergence of new theology, Newell points out that most of the old European churches were built atop sacred wells, a vision of radical immanence and God's presence in nature. As a metaphor, this points to the bedrock and the core. The Divine comes from deep in the earth, unlike much theology that points upward to the heavens as God's dwelling place.

The new theology cannot be constructed by our ego-driven smaller self on the surface. Newell says that we cannot depend on the strength of our ego for transformation in our world:

> The ego claims to be the center but the ego was given to support the center. The work of subtraction of the ego

---

[9] Ken Wilber, *The Religion of Tomorrow* (Boulder, CO: Shambhala, 2017).

[10] Diana Butler Bass and John Philip Newell, "Look Beyond Tradition for New Understanding of God," lecture, Chautauqua Institution, Chautauqua, New York, August 5, 2016.

[11] Bass, *Grounded*, 13.

needs to happen in individuals, nations, religions, even the human species that puts itself at the center of creation.[12]

It is in the questions, in the not-knowing, that learning occurs. We need questions that prompt the imaginative spirit, questions without ready answers, questions that bring about surprise and awe. We need questions like, What is God up to, and what is my purpose? We individually are challenged to create our own story, our own theology, of how God is present in our lives and how we are seeking to be an expression of what God is inviting.[13] A meaningful theology also helps us to make sense of the world as revealed by science.

The Power of Small Groups

Pursuing a deeper religion by cycling to the bedrock of the spirit inevitably means substantial change for institutional religion. The focus of mainline institutions seems to be on the surface, helping parishioners with the quality and direction of their lives and improving the moral culture and social systems they live in.

By focusing on the surface needs of members, religious institutions have set answers to deep questions that need the wisdom of the bedrock. Discussing these questions helps members open their hearts to serving the larger community and deepen their spiritual identity.

Religious institutions and their leaders take people as they come, love them unconditionally, comfort them, and nurture them in their next step toward the bedrock. In this sense transformation is not an institutional movement; it is a personal, relational one.

Small groups in faith communities can be the catalyst for change. Even small unstructured beginnings of relationships can lead to large and unpredictable outcomes. Orchestrating

---

[12] John Philip Newell, "In the Beginning Was the Sound," sermon, The Chautauqua Institution, Chautauqua, New York, August 3, 2016.

[13] Philip Clayton, *Transforming Christian Theology: For Church and Society* (Minneapolis: Fortress Press, 2009).

elaborate events such as strategic planning is likely to have only a small effect on what happens.

As small groups are formed, each group can generate holistic patterns of its own. The groups generally seek ways to lead more purposeful and abundant lives. In this pursuit they inevitably talk about their sense of God and understanding of spirituality. They become intimate communities with flexible and inclusive beliefs that have the potential to influence the holistic pattern of the whole faith community.

If several of these groups journey to the bedrock, they can develop innovations—yeast that can leaven the whole.

For example, I led a sand tray personal growth workshop in which the participants were asked to choose several symbols from an array of objects and talk to their small group about what the symbols meant to them. One man chose a small canoe with a paddle. He said that paddling the canoe represented a new journey. The paddle "that keeps me going in the right direction is my wife," and then he began to cry. The emotion came up suddenly and unexpectedly. For him, that was a sacred moment.

The canoe represented an aspect of his journey—every symbol he chose (a rock, cross, cream can, and tiger) was related to his journey. The story he told had a ripple effect on the group as the members went deeper into their own stories. The Spirit was active in the room, and we all knew it.

No one image or symbol captures the essence of the Spirit. We connect to the Spirit with our own personal images or symbols. These images and symbols are core to the stories of our encounters with the Spirit. These symbols may be related to our recollections, our nostalgia, family, tradition, and culture.

The Spirit powered the cycling of the group through the strata. The autonomous individuals together found a profound truth. They moved beyond a focus on their individual needs to another order of collective being that is union and oneness, autonomy, communion, and connection.

The activism of small groups hold the tension between the traditional church perspective and activism on the surface and what emerges from the deep journey to the collective unconscious in the bedrock.

By going to the bedrock, the small group didn't look for a God who is locked in a doctrinal box on the surface. The bedrock generates new images of the Divine and new symbols of transformation and renewal.

The evolution and sustainability of complex adaptive systems include the natural and necessary processes of destruction and renewal. The creative destruction phase may require dismantling systems and structures on the surface that have become too rigid, have too little variety, and are not responsive to the current needs of the community.[14]

People may cling to the old ways because of past success like financial support, attractive buildings, and the offer of security and certainty about important life-and-death issues. The new worldviews that emerge from the bedrock provide the flexibility to respond to current diversity issues like sexual orientation, race, gender, and socioeconomic class and to see science, technology, social justice, and ecology with new eyes and concern.

A house of worship is a community of relationships bound by love. The community includes all of creation, with the animals who share life on the planet as well as forests, rivers, oceans, and the earth itself. Everything is connected. As Bass states:

> Relational community [webs of relationships], intentional practice [imitating Jesus with deliberation], and experiential belief [in the God we encounter through one another and in the world] are forming a new vision of what it means to be Christian in the twenty-first century. . . . We are; we act; we know.[15]

Interspirituality

The interfaith initiatives of the late twentieth century have opened dialogues and shared wisdom among leaders and practitioners of different religions. These initiatives can flower into exciting new

---

[14] Brenda Zimmerman, Curt Lindberg, and Paul Plsek, *Edgeware: Insights from Complexity Science for Health Care Leaders* (Irving, TX: VHA, 1998), 171.

[15] Diana Butler Bass, *Christianity after Religion: The End of Church and the Birth of a New Spiritual Awakening* (New York: HarperOne, 2013), 214.

possibilities for spiritual exploration and expression.[16] The late Wayne Teasdale, author of *The Mystic Heart,* coined the term *interspirituality* to describe this new spiritual perspective.[17]

Beneath the diversity of theological beliefs, rites, and observances lies a deeper unity of experience of mystical spirituality that is our shared spiritual heritage. Every authentic spiritual path offers unique perspectives and rich insights into this deeper, direct experience of truth. In our time, the wisdom and depth of all paths are available to anyone who brings an open mind, generous spirit, and loving heart to the search across traditions.

All authentic spiritual paths, at their mystical core, are committed to the common values of peace, compassionate service, and love for all creation. An inner life awakened to responsibility and love naturally expresses itself through engaged spirituality, in "acts of compassion . . . , contributing to the transformation of the world and the building of a nonviolent, peace-loving culture that includes everyone."[18]

At the heart of all the questions raised by religion is an energy that comes from deep within the bedrock where nothing is separate, and that everything in our universe is profoundly and inextricably interconnected.

Teasdale writes:

> The real religion of humankind can be said to be spirituality itself, because mystical spirituality is the origin of all the world religions. If this is so, and I believe it is, we might also say that interspirituality—the sharing of ultimate experiences across traditions—is the religion of the third millennium. Interspirituality is the foundation that can prepare the way for a planet-wide enlightened culture, and a continuing community among the religions that is substantial, vital, and creative.[19]

---

[16] Kurt Johnson and David Robert Ord, *The Coming Interspiritual Age* (Vancouver, BC: Namaste Publishing, 2013).

[17] Wayne Teasdale, *The Mystic Heart: Discovering a Universal Spirituality in the World's Religion* (Novato, CA: New World Library, 1999, 2001).

[18] Ibid.

[19] Ibid., 26.

Convergence of Science and Religion

Ken Wilber points out:

> One thing is certain: any spirituality that can't pass mus-
> ter with science will not make it past the modern and
> post-modern tests for truth, and any science that doesn't
> include some components of testable spirituality will
> never find an answer to the ultimate questions of human
> existence.[20]

The World religions have provided tangible ways (places,
times, objects, or persons) that ground us and keep us from
being overwhelmed by the awesome powers of nature and the
universe. Both science and religion make us aware that the
sacred is here and now, in images, in our breath, in our daily
work and play.

Religion gives meaning to the whole of our lives by directing
us to the divinity "at the heart of life itself. How we respond
to this divine lure is how we live in the dynamic energy of
catholicity."[21]

Religion also helps us to embrace the uncertainty that is inherent in nature. It helps us find deep conviction within ourselves,
develop a sense of personal wholeness, make connections with
others, and deepen our connections with the wider world.

Religion lets us see the wholeness in the scattered parts of
our lives.

As we learn more about the bedrock, we realize that amid
the strange movements of quantum energy, there is an order
that also pervades the universe. Religion and science together
help us to make sense of that order and learn about who we
are. We can identify our blind spots and imperfections, develop
compassion, integrity, wisdom, and know what it means to be
human.

The new integration of faith and reason must be "psychologi-
cally relevant, nondogmatic," unconfined by any given religion's

---

[20] Wilber, *The Religion of Tomorrow*, 78.
[21] Ilia Delio, *Making All Things New: Catholicity, Cosmology, Consciousness* (Maryknoll, NY: Orbis Books, 2015), 70.

physical worldview, and self-critical, "able to entertain doubt when necessary." It "includes the intuition or insight that there is another level of reality beyond our ordinary perception of the world."[22]

The intense feeling that there is an external dimension of spirit, something wholly other that we name God, is a "profound energy" in the universe that is also described by science. "Only what is *experientially true* is worthy of a mature spirituality. Experiential spirituality will stretch us, sometimes test us, but will always ask us to be larger than we wish to be."[23]

Is God the creative activity or the One who is responsible for the creative activity? Are God and the creative activity one and the same? Is there a singular eternal reality, One, a power, above, beneath, beyond, and near all? These are questions that can't be resolved by either science or theology, but both science and theology can be informed by each other. The scientist can value religion's perspective on the mystery and divinity in what science studies. Theologians can learn from science about new ways to image the Divine, the Infinite.

In the circuitry of the brain and in the emergent possibilities in the bedrock there is an encounter with the Infinite. When we have such experiences we are pointing at the same ineffable, mysterious, wondrous thing that for millennia we have named God.

Conclusion

The wholeness story helps us to transcend boundaries of science, religion, and spirituality. Both the myths of religion and the laws of science are not so much descriptions of facts as symbols that are expressions of cosmic truths.

The wholeness story is about mystery, myths, and the infinite, eternal consciousness that is in the universe. The wholeness metaphors in the story disorganize "the common sense of things—

---

[22] Lionel Corbett, *Psyche and the Sacred: Spirituality beyond Religion* (New Orleans: Spring Journal, 2012), 208, 215.

[23] Hollis, *Finding Meaning in the Second Half of Life: How to Finally, Really Grow Up*, 189, 185.

jumbling together the abstract with the concrete, the physical with the psychological, the like with the unlike."[24]

As we live the wholeness story with its quantum mysteries, Catherine Keller believes that we may "see more and more theological questions irrupting at the cutting edge of science. . . . The conversations will continue to teeter on the brink of the impossible, as the contradictions of method, specialization, and sensibility will not soon soften."[25]

I believe the conversation will move us to a higher level of consciousness about the mystery, suffering, and complexity of life and build our collective confidence that we can step into the next moment, however unpredictable it may be.

---

[24] James Geary, I Is An Other: The Secret Life of Metaphor and How It Shapes the Way We See the World (New York: Harper, 2011).

[25] Catherine Keller, Cloud of the Impossible: Negative Theology and Planetary Entanglement (New York: Columbia University Press, 2015), 165.

Chapter 10

Deep Community

In this chapter I explore the barriers to creating and sustaining wholeness at the societal level, holistic methods of change, and some simple rules to actualize societal wholeness.

Current Crises

There is a real possibility that the forces we humans have set in motion could destroy the capacity of the earth to regenerate. Unlike the previous destructions of life on earth, this existential threat is from the human species. It is not the impact of an asteroid. We are doing ourselves in.

Raised global temperatures through emission of CO2 gases, methane release, exponential population growth, acidified oceans, and depleted land resources are manifestations of the threat. There is rampant corruption, extreme poverty, ISIS beheadings, and atomic bombs in the hands of psychopaths. The list could go on.

Where did we go wrong? Is there something amiss in our genetic makeup that causes us to deny harsh reality and pretend that all is well? Are we locked into past paradigms and religious and philosophical codes that keep us from confronting the dark side of the human condition?

Contributing to our individual paralysis in the face of impending doom are powerful institutions, ideological movements, and nation states dedicated to maintaining their power and wealth.

They resist protecting and continuing an ecology that supports our life and social systems.

Nazaretyan, a Russian scholar of "Big History," argues that unless the human mind can develop new mechanisms for regulating strategic meaning-construction and solidarity, planetary civilization may be destroyed during the next decades. He points out that the traditional mechanisms of regulating social aggression, particularly religious or quasi-religious ideologies, are becoming counterproductive.[1]

Many of the crises are linked and compounding our danger. Continuing our present path or reinstituting the past will not be enough. It remains to be seen whether our organizations, citizen groups, and governments will act fast enough to prevent the looming world catastrophes and new catastrophes that may emerge.

The years 2016 and 2017 have been times of fragmentation, brokenness of our political systems, new demands for equality, and existential threats of terrorism. But it has also been a time of experimentation, of developing a new consensus about the constructs of a just society.

Fostering a global mindset about wholeness will provide more effective control and regulation over our evolving technologies, weapons, and socially aggressive organizations and societies.

Instead of amplifying group identities to maintain viabilities of societies, applications of the wholeness and cycle of becoming models break down tribal barriers that alienate and demonize the Other. Unlike traditional and fundamental religions and ideologies that demand blind faith and enhance group identity by promoting fear of the present and other-worldly hope for the future, wholeness focuses on positive living in the present and tolerance and compassion for adherents of different faiths and worldviews. A focus on wholeness also meets the emotional and psychological needs of individuals for security amid uncertainty, multiple truths, and a lack of ultimate purpose and meaning.

---

[1] A. P. Nazaretyan, "Life's Meaning as a Global Problem of Modernity: A View from Big History and Complexity Studies Perspective," *Journal of Globalization Studies* (November 2010).

Is Technology Creating the Future?

Based on his analysis of key technological indexes—the speed of microprocessors, the falling cost of transistors, the falling cost of sequencing DNA, the rising number of Internet hosts and nanotechnology patents, Kurzwell argues that technological progress will continue its exponential growth because it has two unbounded resources: "the growing order of the technology itself and the chaos from which an evolutionary process draws its options for further diversity."[2]

Kevin Kelly brilliantly presents an argument about the consequences of this exponential growth of technology: He describes the cloud of machine intelligence, linking billions of human minds in a single supermind of unimagined complexity. This new creation provides a new way of thinking and a new mind for our species. Kelly calls this connectivity the "holos," which includes "the collective intelligence of all humans combined with the collective behavior of all machines, plus the intelligence of nature, plus whatever behavior emerges from this whole." This is a new state, a different world with new normals. This new state that connects all humans and all machines into a global matrix is a "standing wave of change that steadily spills forward new arrangements of our needs and desires."[3]

Kelly's analysis is compelling. Just as many of the evolutionary forces on the planet that affect our lives are beyond our control, the evolution of technology appears to be a process that is creating our future, with or without our consent.

While we experience the "results" of a connection to the Internet with our laptop computer, that experience is possible only because of connections with many servers all over the world. Our activity at the computer contributes to the results, and the result is constructed by our connections. The Internet may be actualizing what Carl Jung described as the universal unconscious, the

---

[2] Ray Kurzwell, *The Age of Spiritual Machines* (New York: Penguin, 1999), 35.

[3] Kevin Kelly, *The Inevitable: Understanding the Twelve Technological Forces That Will Shape Our Future* (New York: Penguin Publishing Group, 2016), 291–96.

presence of a set of images and their significance that is shared by all people.

The Internet is an effort toward the universal unity we yearn for. The Internet has forced a sense of human unity by providing a way to facilitate our continual growth and development. It provides choices for us and others to be creative, for doing well, and for maximizing our gifts and talents. The Internet provides new ways of thinking about the wholeness of the dimensions of body, mind, and soul.

Ilia Delio offers Teilhard's hope that technology will bring about human unity. Yet, with all its potential, the Internet, along with other advanced technology, could sink humanity into an era of meaninglessness without the guidance of religion. If we think of love as a cosmological force, through love and the new technology we can reach a new level of consciousness. Delio expands on the importance of spirituality in the next stage of evolution.

> Teilhard says love is deeply written in the heart of nature and when that love is thwarted, when that love is distorted, we will seek new ways, unconsciously or consciously, to restore that love to a life-giving direction. And that's at the heart of AI technology.
>
> Teilhard de Chardin places God at the center of that process. He calls him "the Omega" from which all love and consciousness arises. Technology will lead to new forms of the sacred, but whatever form it takes, spirituality must be present in the next stage of evolution. Right now, people have developed a hyper-organized left brain, but they've neglected the spiritual right brain, and if they continue to ignore it, humans may extend their lives while draining its meaning.
>
> Knowledge can get us to new places, but love brings us [to the] threshold of another universe.[4]

---

[4] Ilia Delio, "Warning against Transhuman Not Informed by Love, Spiritual Guidance," lecture, Chautauqua Institution, Chautauqua, New York, August 15, 2016.

Resolving Barriers to Societal Wholeness

Conflict on the surface is inevitable. There are major differences of worldviews and vast inequalities of wealth. The media have amplified these differences. The pace of change is without precedent. Public and private leaders and institutions have failed to keep up. Trust in these leaders and institutions is at an all-time low.

Fear and anxiety from the middle drives many of these conflicts. Using the wholeness and the cycle of becoming models develops understanding of the deeper factors affecting these issues and why it is necessary to go to the bedrock to find a resolution.

The wholeness model provides a critique of any culture that dominates its people, that favors one group over another, and that limits human development. The model suggests that as more people, groups, and societies cycle to the bedrock, our unique gifts and talents will transform the earth with love and kindness. Ken Wilber shares this optimistic belief: "Knowing that the entire Creative Force of the whole Kosmos is your constant companion."[5]

At the bedrock there are archetypal forces that excite the middle emotions and affect the ego conflicts on the surface. When we encounter the archetypal forces in the bedrock, we tap into sources of energy, power, and love. These sources have the potential to transform surface conflicts.

> This is at once intoxicating and disturbing. Jung describes contact with the archetypal dimension of the psyche as analogous to touching a high-voltage cable: One feels positively charged with life energy and intoxicating life power.[6]

To make substantial transformations and resolve conflicts on the surface we must access the "multitude of imaginal mysterious

---

[5] Ken Wilber, *The Religion of Tomorrow* (Boulder, CO: Shambhala, 2017), 663.

[6] Keiron Le Grice, *Archetypal Reflection: Insights and Ideas from Jungian Psychology* (New York: Muswell Hill Press, 2016), 29.

and breathtaking moments"[7] in the bedrock. In the bedrock, there is light and illumination, which gives us the possibility of moving beyond cause and effect and beyond the stereotyping and the locked-in positions on the surface that produce the conflicts we experience.

At a time in our nation's life when we are collectively experiencing unresolved conflict, grief, and loss, it is an opportune time to see what archetypes in the bedrock underlie these experiences and how we can harness the light, healing, meaning, and wisdom to change our course on the surface. If we do not, we face the precipice of environmental destruction, war, and unremitting tribal divisions.

Heightening the tension between our collective ego-driven consciousness and our collective unconscious can bring about a shift in our collective resolve to take corrective action on the surface.

These archetypes deep in the bedrock of body, mind, and soul have been there as a form of intelligence since the beginning of time. These forces are unleashed when our collective ego suffers a loss, and we are groping for meaning and solace. We become open to what bubbles up from the bedrock. This can be good or bad, depending on what we do with what emerges. If we can reconcile these insights with our ego consciousness at the surface, we can create heaven on earth. If they only strengthen our paranoia, fear, and anxieties, they can create hell on earth—witness the tyranny of the Nazis and the brutal regimes we can name since the beginning of civilization.

For example, when we interact with the imaginal figures that come to us in our dreams, we can contain the energy and obtain some degree of healing and a sense of connection to solid ground. Harrell describes this process as part of our personal individuation (see Chapter 2) and suggests how these are collective forces that move groups, communities, and nations.[8] An analogy to the Star Wars movies is appropriate. There is a dark side of the Force. But there is also light in the darkness. If we

---

[7] Mary Harrell, *Imaginal Figures in Everyday Life: Stories from the World between Matter and Mind* (Asheville, NC: InnerQuest Books, 2015), 14.

[8] Ibid., 69–72.

activate this power, we can resolve the complex social issues on the surface.

If, as a nation, we don't own and examine our deeply embedded unconscious societal attitudes that gives rise to the violence, racism, sexism, and homophobia on the surface, we are in peril in the short term. In the longer term, if we don't acknowledge our deep suppressed feeling of alienation and abandonment, then our pursuit of wealth, technological prowess, and consumer satiation will do us in. We need to deeply reflect on our issues and problems on the surface to find resolution in the bedrock.

The wealth and wisdom of the bedrock is always there. It has been there waiting for us to find it—it only takes our imagination to find meaning.

Rather than remaining in a state of perpetual conflict on the surface, as we integrate wisdom from the bedrock we can turn conflict into productive, sustainable dialogue and conversation. We can listen to what emerges from the bedrock and notice how it merges with our feelings in the middle. What does it want? Our unconscious is our best teacher. If we deal with that fully, a third possibility will emerge, one that embraces both our intuition and our position on the surface. We need to be open to the surprise and what wants to come in.

Hope for Holistic Change in Society

There is not a best or only way of achieving a wholeness of body, mind, and soul. We can find wisdom in the physical realm where living cells count on quantum activity to maintain life, in our consciousness where our intuitive powers can imagine holistic solutions to problems beyond our analytic minds, to the bedrock of our soul where we find the grace and love that transcends our worldly concerns. At the bedrock of all three dimensions we find a sense of the sacred, the spirit of the Divine at work. Capturing this sense of wholeness is essential to understanding a way out of our ecological, social, and political quandary.

This sacred wholeness is immanent in everything we do, in every transaction we make, in every relationship we develop. The cycle of becoming illustrates that our lives require continuous movement from the surface through the turbulent middle to the bedrock and return to renew and reenergize our lives on the surface. The cycling restores meaning to our daily lives and enables practices that contribute to a sustainable world.

As we enter the bedrock, we encounter the light of God. We enter the imaginal world to a new creation, a new vision, a sense that we are connected to all that matters, to everything we need, to a new story, to wholeness. When we dwell in the bedrock, as we explore more, know more, understand more, and love more, we see what is good and beautiful.

The story of the universe sees life in a continuous process of transcending itself and moving in a biased trajectory toward an increase in beauty, truth, and goodness. The earth has been through a great many cataclysmic events and has managed to come through each one with even more resilience and intelligence. Bruce Sanguin says that when we align ourselves with the impulse to evolve, "we are aligning ourselves with the very heart of God."[9]

In nature, there is condensation and evaporation, hibernation and waking up, the four seasons, the life cycles of everything, and even the constant birth of stars that create the elements that formed us. There is constant death and resurrection. Delio says:

> There is an unbearable and unstoppable energy at the heart of the cosmos that is relentless, despite billions of years of cosmic life. This yearning for wholeness is integral to the unfinished process of evolution because it is an ultimate wholeness that exceeds the human grasp. God is the unbearable wholeness of being, the unrelenting dynamism of love, pushing through the limits of matter to become God at the heart of this evolutionary universe. Divine love evolves the universe as it leans into an unknown future.[10]

---

[9] Bruce Sanguin, "Evolutionary Spirituality—Tenet 2," blog, February 22, 2015.

[10] Ilia Delio, *The Unbearable Wholeness of Being: God, Evolution, and the Power of Love* (Maryknoll, NY: Orbis Books, 2013), 202.

Coherence, as explained by the quantum biologists, is that state in the bedrock of living cells where the quantum possibilities—electrons being everywhere at once—are essential for life. Accessing the coherence in the bedrock of our mind and soul is essential for flourishing mentally and spiritually.

Ervin Laszlo argues that there is a deep reality in the cosmos that connects and creates coherence that makes moral action possible. He believes that the behavior we choose (on the surface) "can be considered moral to the extent that it contributes to the coherence of the subject, and to the coherence of the world around the subject."[11]

Nonhuman species such as the great apes are generally coherent as they instinctively maintain or improve community integrity and well-being. "Creating incoherence through unnecessary aggression, violence, and irrational fragmentation and polarization is a uniquely human trait."[12] However, we can also recognize that incoherence-inducing behavior is counter-functional. We can also choose to act to maintain the health, integrity, and coherence of body, mind, and soul as well as of the environment and society.

John Haught believes that to find coherence we need to look to the future.

> God is present as a gracious horizon of "futurity" that keeps inviting the universe, in ways that are always mysterious, to keep moving deeper into the territory of the "not-yet." God acts not by forcing the world mechanically and coercively from behind, but by opening up the past and present in new modes of being from up ahead. God acts not by absorbing, dissolving, or overwhelming the present world, but by "going before" it as an endless reservoir of future opportunities for new being. . . .
>
> If God's love works by opening creation to a new future, then, our own vocation is similarly to open up a new future for everything and everyone we profess to love. Love

---

[11] Ervin Laszlo, *Quantum Shift in a Global Brain: How the New Science of Reality Can Change Us and Our World* (Rochester, VT: Inner Traditions, 2008), 110–11, 119.

[12] Ibid., 120.

flourishes most fully and effectively, therefore, only where there is a sustained—indeed intergenerational expectation that something really big awaits *all things* up ahead.[13]

Simple Rules for Creating the Future

Complex issues on the surface threaten to consume us. Unless we use holistic models like the wholeness model, we will be locked into a linear oversimplified model of society driven by our egoistic small selves on the surface. We need to cycle through the strata to develop new understandings of what it means to be human, resist dehumanizing strategies, and watch for alternative and novel ways of dealing with issues that emerge on the surface.

What emerges is likely to follow new rules that often cannot be derived from the behavior of the parts that make up the whole. The new rules will be derived from an integration of the wisdom of the body, mind, and soul.

Meaning, universe, spirit, God, creation and all other abstract concepts are themselves ideas that took form over countless generations as people shared their aspirations to understand and express what may lie beyond the visible world. This emergent phenomenon has created the power of all our words and ideas, including ideals like truth, justice, and freedom, which took millennia to clarify in practice, and which no individual could ever have invented or even imagined without a rich cultural history that made doing so possible.

The wholeness model presents an adaptive capacity to learn. Learning and development persists, beginning with a knowledge of self and others, making sense of the environment, and making connections to learn and evolve. In this common capacity to adapt there are some simple rules that we follow. Although expressed in different language and symbols, the simple rules offer a guide to self-knowledge, learning about what is happening, and development of strategies to evolve.[14]

---

[13] John Haught, "Love, Hope, and the Cosmic Future," Omega Center blog, January 16, 2017.

[14] Mallary Tydell and Royce Holladay, *Simple Rules: A Radical Inquiry into Self* (Apache Junction, AZ: Gold Canyon Press, 2011).

Simple rules shape the conditions that generate the patterns of our lives. If we want to change these patterns, focusing on a simple rule will create conditions for the patterns to change. Simple rules set the boundaries of what actions we will take while leaving ample scope for flexibility within those limits. Religion has traditionally created rules that constrain our behavior.

The simple rules we follow as we cycle through the strata create the underlying dynamics that generate and sustain our coherent patterns on the surface. We can develop the rules individually in reflection and meditation. Or, collectively, we can make explicit or implicit agreements about the conditions that will set the patterns in our group, organization, or community.

The simple rules facilitate convergence and coherence. They provide a path for cycling, often called the "Way" in many religious, spiritual, and humanist traditions. By understanding and working with simple rules, we can develop greater adaptive mental capacities based on both the material and nonmaterial and transcendent aspects of our own reality and the reality of others. Knowing the rules that guide our life helps us to make an intelligent presentation of religious faith, present a coherent view of empirical reality, and live a spiritual and emotionally satisfying life (most of the time). Three simple rules I suggest are:

1. Recognize the boundaries, limitations, and strengths of your current worldview

The boundaries of knowledge are expanding. Paradigms are changing along with methods and theories that push the frontiers of each domain. With new discoveries come the realization that much is unknown. Our worldviews are subject to change as fragments of data or experience are united to create new entities, "a deepening of being that is a deepening of love."[15]

2. Recognize the significance of what is emerging

There is an energy and force in the universe that constantly self-organizes our understanding of what is important. Our challenge

---

[15] Ilia Delio, *Making All Things New: Catholicity, Cosmology, Consciousness* (Maryknoll, NY: Orbis Books, 2015), 146.

is to focus on what is significant in the current moment. The dimensions of body, mind, and soul are interacting, and the spirit is moving from surface to bedrock. The material is not separate from the mystical. We cannot exclude either as unimportant.

3. Make broad and deep connections to transforming relationships

We cannot live fully unless we are in a relationship with something outside our selves—another person, an idea, a place, or a situation. We must continually recognize our interdependence with both our social world and the natural world and choose relationships that transform us.

These three simple rules help us to understand that when we experience something that transcends our understanding of the ordinary world, whether in nature, in dreams, or in the context of a religious setting, we sense it as the divine manifesting through us. These experiences often produce a sense of oneness, a union with the earth or other people and creatures, or even radical change in our thinking or actions. When we hold the tension between our current experience on the surface and what we experience in the bedrock, a new understanding emerges.

Holding the tension of opposites is the "transcendent function"[16] that is the core of Carl Jung's theory of psychological growth and the heart of what he called "individuation," the process by which one is guided in a teleological way toward the person one is meant to be.

The transcendent function opens a dialogue between the conscious and unconscious to allow a living, third thing to emerge that is neither a combination of nor a rejection of the two. It has a central role in the self-regulating nature of the psyche and the self's drive toward wholeness. It may be an expression of a larger human urge to reconcile ontological quandaries such as spirit and matter, subject and object, inner and outer, idea and thing, form and substance, thought and feeling. Viewed in this way,

---

[16] Edwin E. Olson, "The Transcendent Function in Organization Change," *Journal of Applied Behavioral Science* 26 (1990): 69–81.

the transcendent function can be thought of as an archetypal phenomenon that is inherent in human experience.

> The transcendent function can be used as a tool for everyday living, to prompt a conversation between that which is known/conscious/acknowledged and that which is unknown/unconscious/hidden, a dialogue through which something new emerges. . . . The essence of the transcendent function is to allow something new to emerge from things that are in seemingly irreconcilable conflict. Through these concepts, the transcendent function is applicable to relationships, social and cultural issues . . . and day-to-day living. . . . The transcendent function allows us to see all the world as a way of embodying, relating to, and integrating the unconscious.[17]

Conclusion

As an aid to our transformation from a linear, cause-and-effect worldview to a holistic view of the connectedness of everything, the wholeness model can be a container for seeing and experiencing belonging, connection, interdependence, and perpetual change.

The model raises questions rather than provides answers. The questions about conditions on the surface move people to confront difficult emotions in the middle and then to find wisdom in the bedrock.

If we sustain our connection to the bedrock, we can make moral decisions not out of fear but out of the coherence of our larger self. When enough people are in this state of connection to the bedrock, there can be significant stabilization and progress toward wholeness in the collective. We will grasp the dynamics of catholicity and the making of the whole to expand our own authentic potential.

---

[17] Jeffrey C. Miller, *The Transcendent Function: Jung's Model of Psychological Growth through Dialogue with the Unconscious* (Albany: SUNY Press, 2004), 8.

The quest for wholeness, whether on an individual, group, or societal level, takes time. It is an intentional process, like practicing the piano. Jungian analyst Murray Stein says that wholeness "is won anew each day . . . one day builds on another . . . each day is a brand new struggle" to attain the results one wants. Psychological wholeness is "to practice living on several levels at the same time."[18]

We are living a dream—a rational, analytic, ego-driven dream—that we have concocted on the surface. For a new, transformative dream, we must go to our individual and collective unconscious as native people have done for centuries. Our new vision must come from deep within.

---

[18] Murray Stein, *Practicing Wholeness: Analytical Psychology and Jungian Thought* (New York: Continuum, 1996), 11–12.

Epilogue

Reflection after Writing This Book

While writing the final chapters in this book I had a series of brief dreams that I interpreted as both caution and encouragement about my process.

> I create a garden, a labyrinth for people to learn about something. A friend, a black male, has developed a cure for a bug infestation of leaves. I try to help him to find someone in the science field to verify it. There is a lot of resistance, even ridicule, about this solution since it was made with common ingredients. I know that his solution is effective.

> I am grading a paper by John. His first paper was a "B." I give him an "A" on this one because it was well organized and made references back and forth in the book.

> I am at a reception with a group of faculty members who ask questions about the book I am writing. Some are skeptical about using quantum biology since I am not a scientist. My responses are very lucid and clear.

The impact of the dreams was to remind me of my shortcomings and need for humility as I put forth my ideas. I believe I am self-aware, but my life is often disordered and in need of the corrections and grace I find in my bedrock of dreams and the feedback I receive from my friends. I need to be reminded of the impact my work may have on others and their need for proof, certainty, and coherence. I need to hold lightly my claims for relevance and usefulness of the wholeness and cycle of becoming models, even though I claim they are only strong metaphors.

Our body, mind, and soul are amazingly complex. I know that other ways to explore wholeness may be more effective for some readers. What I have written is at best incomplete. I am open to adjusting my views as new revelations about theology, quantum biology, and the mysteries of life come to the fore. I need to continue my engagement with scientists, theologians, and interested readers of all persuasion who understand reality in different ways.

New Good News

When I was growing up, the Christian gospel was called the good news, the good news of Jesus Christ. In recent years, as I have become more spiritual, more mystical, and more in sync with a scientific understanding of reality, I have realized that the good news of the gospel is a foundation of new good news.

My explorations in writing this book have taken me further into the depths of how the physical world, our intelligence, and our faith in a transcendent Spirit—everything—are integrated. They are three dimensions of one Reality that has multiple strata which quantum biologists have grouped into three: the *surface* reality of our traditional world of objects and classical laws of physics and nature; a *middle* stratum where there is turbulence, noise, emotions, and our striving to know ultimate Reality; and a *bedrock* stratum where our traditional understandings no longer apply. At the bedrock we encounter a deep wisdom, the light and love of God, and a wave of quantum possibilities, a stratum where things happen beyond our ability to understand or explain.

In this book I have argued that it is necessary to go beyond the edge of the surface and the middle to get into the bedrock. I have been led even further to the mystery beneath and before the bedrock—the mystery of the absolute darkness, chaos, and silence I have labeled the *core*.

At each stratum the Spirit is moving, creating moments that cycle across the dimensions and through the strata, bringing me to the depths of the bedrock and beyond for renewal and then lifting me up to the surface, renewed and strengthened to be the body of Christ in the world, sanctified and transformed.

This is the new good news that helps me to understand what is happening in the world, to not despair but rather to live in the hope that, over time, individuals, groups, and societies with different faiths and traditions will learn and grow from their journeys through the dimensions and strata of the one Reality.

Glossary

This is a list of some of the concepts of science and religion as they are used in this book. The meanings may differ, at least in part, from those used conventionally.

Active imagination facilitates an inward journey to the bedrock by a process of conscious dialogue with the unconscious. As in prayer and meditation, the practice of active imagination is receptive to whatever comes up from the bedrock, but unlike prayer and meditation, a person can engage with the image of the person or object that has emerged.

Antenarratives are alternative constructions of reality on the surface stratum. The antenarrative generates viewpoints that reflect the interplay between dominant narratives and the antenarrative resulting in a more complex perception of reality equal to the complexity of a rapidly changing environment.

Archetypes are formative principles in the unconscious of the mind dimension that animate and condition our life experience. The fundamental forms of the archetypes are essentially unknowable, lying beyond the limits of the psyche. In the wholeness model the archetypal forms in the bedrock constellate in the middle as emotions and drives; on the surface they take form as symbols. The archetypes are universal determinants, but they are affected by the cultural context (surface) and by the personal experience and personality of the individual,

Authority is one of the four ways of knowing. This knowledge is expressed in the surface stratum as conventional wisdom, ethics, and moral knowledge that rely on commonly accepted *external*

authorities (codes, scriptures, laws, or other people). In more recent times there has been a shift to relying on *internal* authority.

Bedrock stratum is a quantum state where space and time are not relevant. The atoms and molecules in the body dimension, our dreams in the mind dimension, and our spiritual experiences in the soul dimension reside there. The interactions in this stratum harness the energy of quantum possibilities and the deep wisdom in the bedrock to activate the middle and surface strata and add to the diversity of life. There are many interpretations and explanations of what exactly happens at the bedrock stratum, but in this book I argue that the phenomena are the same, at least metaphorically.

The **body dimension** is one of the three dimensions of the wholeness model. It includes all aspects of life that affect our physical well-being, including the cells and organs of our bodies in the surface stratum, the thermodynamic layer of liquids and gases in the middle stratum, and the atoms and molecules and their particles in the bedrock stratum (which obey the precise and reliable rules of quantum mechanics).

Catholicity is the ever-evolving process of life that creates coherence. When we are coherent at the bedrock, we have health and integrity. We are whole and attend to the "big picture," the world beyond ego-gratification.

The **cloud of possibility** is an interconnection between apophatic theology and quantum physics at the bedrock. Both domains speak of pure possibility and radical indeterminacy where events that take place very far apart seem to be entangled because "both events form a single creative act, a single 'actual entity' arising out of a common field of potentialities." (Catherine Keller, *Cloud of Impossibility*)

Code-switching, used often by minority members of a group in daily life, means modifying behavior, appearance, language, mannerisms, and so forth on the surface stratum to adapt to different sociocultural norms.

Coherence occurs at the molecular level in the body dimension where biological processes are very fast (trillionths of a second) and are confined to short atomic distances, when atoms are doing all of the quantum behavior of tunneling, superposition, and entanglement—a circumstance where large numbers of particles cooperate. As an analogy, we can think of water molecules forming waves in the ocean or the neurons in our brain linking together to form a coherent thought.

The collective unconscious, a term originating with Carl Jung, refers to structures of the unconscious mind that are shared among beings of the same species. The human collective unconscious is populated by instincts and by archetypes, universal symbols such as the Great Mother, the Wise Old Man, the Shadow, Paradise, the Tree of Life, and many more.

Consciousness is a process of perpetual development. We are aware of the shifting patterns of our life when we are awake. We experience a succession of continuous moments that become and dissolve. We intentionally or unintentionally link these moments together in patterns to create our conscious reality. While awake, images and ideas come and go and combine and recombine, sometimes unpredictably. When asleep, our unconscious mind descends into the unknown, the irrational, and the illuminated source at the bedrock. The causation and meaning assigned in the conscious state dissolves.

The core is not in the quantum biology model of life, but I include it in the wholeness model because this is the realm of mystery, the source, the unknowable, the initial void, silence, and darkness before the development of quanta and the beginning of time and space as we know it. This could be the Big Bang, Apophatic Divinity, or an infinity of chaos, randomness, and uncertainty.

Creative emergence is a self-organizing space in which the information from the four ways of knowing blend and emerge as a pattern or order people experience and express in their roles as writer, artist, dancer, worker, student, and so on. The new knowledge flows through the person, not from the person.

The **cycle of becoming** (Figure 3–1) is actually three cycles in the wholeness model. The first is a cycle between the surface and middle. What happens at the surface triggers positive or negative sensation or emotions in the middle. Conversely, what is happening in the middle affects our life on the surface, either positively or negatively. The second cycle is between the surface and the bedrock. This will always have a positive outcome because the love and wisdom in the bedrock serves the best interest of the self on the surface. The third cycle is between the surface and the core. This may be a frequent cycle for those who are spiritually aware, but a cycle less taken by those locked into the ego on the surface.

Cycling is the repeating movement through the strata of the wholeness model in all facets of our lives. Cycling creates a progression that can also be viewed as spiraling into a future of greater complexity. Cycling enables us to tune in to the changes that are happening to ourselves, to close friends, our neighbors, our nation, and indeed the whole world. If we don't continually cycle, our worldviews and interpretations of events inevitably become fossilized and do not adapt to current realities.

"Dance" is the process, necessary for life to survive on the surface stratum, whereby living cells harness the thermodynamic molecular noise in the middle stratum to maintain, rather than disrupt, quantum coherence. Metaphorically, body, mind, and soul must "dance" with the molecules, feelings, and meditations in the middle strata to reach coherence in the bedrock. "Dance" implies that there is an element of randomness and uncertainty that enables the emergence of novelty.

Decoherence is the "leaking away" of coherence. All atoms interact with trillions of other atoms all the time. This complex interaction causes the delicate coherence to leak away very quickly and be lost in the incoherent noise of its surroundings in the middle stratum. A cell dies when its connection with the orderly quantum realm is severed, leaving it powerless to resist the forces of the thermodynamic middle stratum.

Deep ecology is a philosophy of nature that sees the environmental crisis as a symptom of a psychological or spiritual disconnection from the bedrock that afflicts modern humanity. This philosophy holds that humans have an illusion of separation from nature by anthropocentrism or human centeredness. Deep ecology critiques the idea that we are the crown of creation, the measure of all being; that the world is merely a resource, a pyramid with humanity rightly on top; and that nature has instrumental value only.

Depth psychology, the psychology of the unconscious, is a modern way of seeking to connect to the deep powers in the bedrock that are beyond our conscious control. Jung named the deep place as the personal and collective unconscious. Compared to the conscious world at the surface, which we access through our senses and experience, accessing the unconscious requires us to welcome the imaginative and integrative powers of our psyche, as in dreaming.

Dialogue originates as the parties in a conversation at the surface hear one another and share their gifts. A broader perspective and understanding emerges, new channels and pathways are opened, and an inclusive vision is possible. To go deeper into our relationships, to engage the troubling negative emotions in the middle, and to open to the wisdom of the bedrock require a dialogue of inquiry, not judgment.

Dimensions model the three dimensions of body, mind, and soul in the wholeness model. These dimensions are separated to emphasize their differences; however, the dimensions are intertwined in a unity of life, mindfulness, and spirituality. Quantum and nonmaterial processes in our bodies, in our consciousness, and in our spiritual life are united into a coherent whole.

Emergence is the unpredictable result of new combinations and complex relationships of forces and materials in any system without direct, linear action.

Emergent behavior characterizes the biodiversity of the earth, the human mind, the emotions, and the biochemical processes that cannot be understood in terms of simple laws. The emergent behavior in cycling through the strata is unpredictable and irreducible because the interaction of the parts can produce an infinite number of patterns. The human mind, for example, with the interaction of billions of neurons, cannot be predicted.

Emotional granularity is the ability to differentiate between our emotions and the affect each is having on us. Developing this ability helps us to be more agile at regulating our emotions.

Empiricism is one of the four ways of knowing that represents objective reality and truth as verified by evidence.

Entanglement refers to pairs of photons separated by hundreds of miles influencing each other. If all hundred billion neurons in a human brain are entangled, they may be binding together all of the information encoded in separated nerves and providing the conscious mind with the powerful capabilities of a quantum computer.

Epigenetics refers to the carefully orchestrated chemical reactions that activate and deactivate, as we grow and develop, parts of the genome at strategic times and in specific locations. The field of epigenetics explores how external factors such as the environment can change a chromosome without alterations in the DNA sequence.

Epistemology is the philosophy of the grounds of knowledge, including its limits and validity.

Green spirituality is a spirituality of horizontal transcendence. Rather than assume matter is lifeless, a green spirituality sees matter as the source of all the rich and varied phenomena of life and consciousness.

The **group sand tray** exercise helps participants to address specific concerns by building small worlds with miniature figures in a large tray of sand and then sharing the worlds they have created. The method helps to create a strong group bond as well as to evoke a deep sense of empowerment for the individual and the group.

Holism is a focus on whole systems rather than the parts.

Holistic change happens in a positive way as we start to see one another's strengths and build a culture on the surface that supports and empowers those strengths and cares for one another in our weaknesses. The whole universe is composed of self-organizing systems of endless levels of complexity. The catholicity of complex evolving systems leads to the wisdom required to build a better human community on and for our planet.

Holos is the collective intelligence of all humans combined with the collective behavior of all machines, plus the intelligence of nature, plus whatever behavior emerges from this whole on the surface. This is a new state, a different world with new normal connecting all humans and all machines into a "standing wave of change that steadily spills forward new arrangements of our needs and desires." (Kevin Kelly, *The Inevitable*)

Idolatry is the devotion to or worship of a physical object as a god on the surface. Using only one or two ways of knowing about reality may be idolatrous.

Imaginal figures in the soul dimension can be "inner" figures, unique to a particular person, or representations of "outer" figures that are experienced by many. Imaginal figures can be investigated through dream figures, reverie, and active imagination.

Imaginal reality is a dynamic and real place of experience, a bedrock inhabited by multivocal, multivalent beings, including interior figures and images that are neither fully matter nor fully spirit. The soul is the imaginal dimension in between matter (body) and mind.

Individuation in Jungian therapies refers to individuals' transformation by accessing their personal unconscious as well as by bringing the collective unconscious from the bedrock into the consciousness of their personality on the surface.

Insight is one of the four ways of knowing; it combines our intuitive way of perceiving things and our ability to make meaning through our personal experience. This way of knowing includes our ability to "pre-understand" something we may later be able to know theoretically and our ability to sense "something more" from the bedrock that is beyond words and not able to be described by our senses.

Integral theology embodies the emergence of the integral worldview in which the dimensions of reality are seen as multiple reflections of the unfolding process of cosmic evolution. This unifying perspective appreciates the interior dynamics of consciousness and culture that are at play below the surface of every issue. Integral theology describes how we move to higher stages of consciousness, increasing complexity, and a special simplicity that recognizes the whole.

Integrity depends upon claiming the "spine" of our personality, both embracing our strengths and accepting our "shadow," our blind spot. This is the inner basis of the uprightness we look for in ourselves and in each other. When we cycle to the bedrock, we encounter our blind spots, but we also gain insights into the whole of life. When we are sensitive to the needs of the whole, we have integrity.

Interspirituality lies beneath the diversity of theological beliefs, rites, and observances. It is a deeper unity of experience of mystical spirituality in the soul dimension that is our shared spiritual heritage. All authentic spiritual paths, at their mystical core, are committed to the common values of peace, compassionate service, and love for all creation. At the heart of all religions is an energy that comes from deep within the bedrock, where nothing is separate, where everything in our universe is profoundly and inextricably interconnected. Interspirituality is the foundation that can prepare the way for a planet-wide enlightened culture, and a continuing community among the religions that is substantial, vital, and creative.

Keystone species are those that have a disproportionate effect relative to their abundance. If a keystone species is removed from the environment, there is a sharp decline in diversity, many other species become extinct, and one species takes over.

Love-Energy is God's compassion, loving into being that which, as yet, does not exist. Divine love sees the potential, the possible beauty of what could be, and calls it into being.

The **middle stratum** is the stratum immediately beneath the surface. This is the turbulent thermodynamic level of liquids and gases in the body dimension; the emotions, feelings, and desires in the mind dimension; and the spiritual longings in the soul dimension that propel action at the surface.

The **mind dimension** represents the more intangible functional aspects of the brain, the subjective aspects of neural activity as opposed to the brain's "objective" structure, physiological aspects.

Moral agency is an individual's ability to make moral judgments on the surface based on some notion of right and wrong and to be held accountable for these actions. We are all moral role models that influence those around us.

Mysticism means experiential knowledge of spiritual things, as opposed to book knowledge, secondhand knowledge, or seminary or church knowledge. Mystics have moved from belief systems or belonging systems to actual inner experience.

Myth is the deeper meaning of the life we experience.

Narratives contain the conflicts and tensions we experience, the patterns in our life that capture our attention, and our hopes for the future. The cycle of becoming shows how our reality is continuously being constructed from our interactions in and between the three strata of surface, middle, and bedrock, and the three dimensions of body, mind, and soul.

The **Omega Point** is the "point" in creation, theorized Teilhard de Chardin, that draws (or lures) our consciousness to a spiritual level. This could represent the spirit that activates the cycle of becoming.

Onesidedness occurs when we grant absolute status to one or two ways of knowing and thus are kept from seeing and participating in the wholeness of reality. Wholeness emerges when we see the patterns that emerge from the interaction of the four ways of knowing.

Praxis is one of the four ways of knowing. It is our experienced coherence of knowing through acting on our understanding and inner sensation of who and how we are and why we are here. In praxis we enact, practice, and embody a theory or lesson. Ideas and skills are engaged, applied, and realized.

Presence is an awareness of the larger whole, leading to actions that can help to shape our future by sensing the unfolding whole within each of us, within the present situation, and acting in service of it.

Quantum biology describes how life's roots reach down from the cells of living things on the surface through the turbulent middle thermodynamic layer to penetrate the quantum bedrock. This allows life to harness the strange quantum reality to allow enzymes to speed up chemical reactions.

The **quantum biology model of life** (Figure 1–1) shows how life's most fundamental processes depend on a new understanding of the quantum world. The quantum biology model of life at the edge of quantum reality provides a strong metaphor for all aspects of our lives, including our physical being, our conscious awareness, and our sense of a transcendent spirit.

Quantum edge describes a theory of how life navigates a narrow strait between the classical and quantum worlds. Rather than avoiding molecular storms in the middle stratum, life embraces them, like the captain of a ship who harnesses turbulent gusts and squalls to maintain the ship upright and on course. As a result, quantum activity in the bedrock is able to affect life on the surface.

Reality is a framework in which people organize their beliefs around axioms that are contained in the worldviews they have inherited.

Sacred groves are essential in urban areas for maintaining social capital at the sacred-urban nexus. The interdependent exchange between the essential grove and urban life could be considered as an archetype of paradise.

Self refers both to the larger self, which is empowered and not restricted to the demands of the ego, and to our smaller self, which is focused on survival and security. The larger self is driven by a need for self-actualization, serving others, and doing worthwhile things. We have the capacity to transcend our material and social needs and values to achieve a larger self.

Self-organization, when conditions are right, creates order within a system on the surface. A system that is pushed far from equilibrium restructures itself.

Simple rules shape the conditions that generate the patterns of our lives on the surface. If we want to change these patterns, focusing on a simple rule will create new conditions and the patterns will change. Simple rules set the boundaries of what actions we will take while leaving ample scope for flexibility within those limits.

The **soul dimension** is the spiritual reality of what is growing within us as we evolve, a positive, purposeful force at the core of our being.

Strata are three divisions of life: *surface,* the macroscopic world of everyday objects such as the cells of our bodies; *middle,* the thermodynamic layer of liquids and gases in living things; and *bedrock,* the world of atoms and molecules and their particles in everything that obeys the precise and reliable rules of quantum mechanics.

Superposition denotes the phenomena of electrons vanishing from one point in space and instantly materializing at another. Something happening over *here* has an instantaneous effect over *there*, no matter how far away *there* is.

The **surface stratum** is the macro everyday world of physical objects, people, nature, and the universe where physical objects and behavior can be observed, measured, and predicted (at least with known probabilities).

Synchronicity is a strong metaphor for describing how disparate elements without apparent connection are brought together or juxtaposed in a manner that tends to shock or surprise the mind, rendering it open to new possibilities. The recognition of synchronicity takes us to the bedrock, a place of deep mutuality, where ego no longer rules.

The **transcendent function** holds a creative tension between what is happening on the surface and the unknown and unpredictable possibilities in the bedrock, enabling something new to emerge. Holding the tension opens us up to the mediating influences of a transcendent force and the emergence of a transformation. Jung called this mediating force the transcendent function, which is the space or field that mediates between the conscious and unconscious.

Transrational reality describes the nonpersonal, nonrational phenomena occurring in the natural universe. Transrational reality is not explainable by our standard cause-and-effect logical structures. There is also a cultural and psychological bias against transrational experiences, such as dreams. The transrational experience is a sacred mystery connected to the source of life itself, a dimension that preexisted before any concept of a personified deity. This is the essence of the core in the wholeness model.

Tunneling is the quantum process that allows particles in an atom to pass through impenetrable barriers as easily as sound passes through walls. For a particle to quantum tunnel, it must remain in a wave state in order to seep through the barrier. Big objects are made up of trillions of atoms that cannot behave in a coherent wave-like fashion. By quantum standards, living cells are also big objects, so it would seem unlikely that quantum tunneling could occur. But the particles in the interior of an enzyme of a cell are engaged in a choreographed "dance" that makes a difference to life.

The **unconscious** is a massive edifice millions of years in the making. Our unconscious mind contains an amazing array of instincts and adaptations capable of immense creativity. It contains all the basic plans required for life on earth as we evolved in small foraging bands in the ancestral environment. The instincts self-organize and manifest themselves in ways beyond our conscious awareness, although consciousness rests upon the unconscious.

The **ways of knowing** (Figure 5–1) represent reality and truth, albeit from different sources. *Insight* represents subjective reality and the truth of individuals. *Authority* represents normative reality and the truths of a collective of people. *Empiricism* represents objective reality and truth as verified by evidence. *Praxis* represents practical reality and personally integrated truth. All four modes are valuable and necessary for life, but it is from their interaction that deeper levels of knowledge emerge.

Wholeness exists based on the source and foundation of all things. This wholeness encompasses our physical, mental, and spiritual realities. Understanding this dynamic wholeness in the universe deepens both faith and science perspectives.

The **wholeness model** (Figure 1–3) is a method, a tool, to explore the connectedness and possible integration of everything. The model, based on the quantum biology depiction of life, has three dimensions—body, mind, and soul—portrayed in three columns and three strata—surface, middle, and bedrock—which constitute the rows in the model. The core at the bottom of the model represents speculation about what existed before the appearance of quantum particles, consciousness, and even divine presence.

Select Bibliography

Armstrong, Karen. *Twelve Steps to a Compassionate Life.* New York: Anchor Books, 2010.

Bache, Christopher W. *The Living Classroom: Teaching and Collective Consciousness.* Albany: State University of New York (SUNY) Press, 2010.

Bass, Diana Butler. *Grounded: Finding God in the World—A Spiritual Revolution.* New York: HarperCollins.

Corbett, Lionel. *Psyche and the Sacred: Spirituality beyond Religion.* New Orleans: Spring Journal, 2012.

D'Aquili, Eugene C., and Andrew B. Newberg. *The Mystical Mind: Probing the Biology of Religious Experience.* Minneapolis: Fortress Press, 1999.

Delio, Ilia. *The Unbearable Wholeness of Being: God, Evolution, and the Power of Love.* Maryknoll, NY: Orbis Books, 2013.

———. *Making All Things New: Catholicity, Cosmology, Consciousness.* Maryknoll, NY: Orbis Books, 2015.

Dodds, Joseph. *Psychoanalysis and Ecology at the Edge of Chaos: Complexity Theory, Deleuze, Guattari, and Psychoanalysis for a Climate in Crisis.* New York: Routledge, 2011.

Fox, Matthew. *Meister Eckhart: A Mystic Warrior for Our Times.* Novato, CA: New World Library, 2014.

Frank, Adam, *The Constant Fire: Beyond the Science and Religion Debate.* Berkeley and Los Angeles: University of California Press, 2009.

Gergen, Kenneth J. *Relational Being: Beyond Self and Community.* New York: Oxford University Press, 2009.

223

Gleiser, Marcelo. *The Island of Knowledge: The Limits of Science and the Search for Meaning.* New York: Basic Books, 2014.

Goodwyn. Eric D. *The Neurobiology of the Gods: How Brain Physiology Shapes the Recurrent Imagery of Myth and Dreams.* New York: Routledge, 2012.

Goodenough, Ursula. *The Sacred Depths of Nature.* New York: Oxford University Press, 1998.

Griffith, Colleen M. "Underhill's Practical Mysticism: One Hundred Years Later." *NTR* 27, no. 1 (September 2014).

Griffiths, Bede. *A New Vision of Reality: Western Science, Eastern Mysticism, and Christian Faith.* Springfield, IL: Templegate, 1990.

Haisch, Bernard. *The Purpose-Guided Universe: Believing in Einstein, Darwin, and God.* Franklin Lakes, NJ: New Page Books, 2010.

Harrell, Mary. *Imaginal Figures in Everyday Life: Stories from the World between Matter and Mind.* Asheville, NC: InnerQuest Books, 2015.

Harrison, Peter. *The Territories of Science and Religion.* Chicago: University of Chicago Press, 2015.

Haskell, David George. *The Songs of Trees: Stories from Nature's Great Connectors.* New York: Viking, 2017.

Haught, John. *Science and Faith: A New Introduction.* New York: Paulist Press, 2013.

Herzfeld, Noreen. *Technology and Religion: Remaining Human in a Co-Created World.* West Conshocken, PA: Templeton Press, 2010.

Hollis, James, *Finding Meaning in the Second Half of Life: How to Finally, Really Grow Up.* New York: Avery, 2006.

———. *Haunting: Dispelling the Ghosts Who Run Our Lives.* Asheville, NC: Chiron Publications, 2013.

Houston, Jean. *The Search for the Beloved: Journeys in Sacred Psychology.* Los Angeles: Jeremy P. Tarcher, 1987.

Johnson, Elizabeth. *Quest for the Living God: Mapping Frontiers in the Theology of God.* New York: Continuum, 2007.

Johnson, Kurt, and David Robert Ord. *The Coming Interspiritual Age.* Vancouver, BC: Namaste Publishing, 2013.

Jung, Carl G. *Memories, Dreams, Reflections.* New York: Vintage Books, 1989 <1961>.

———. "Individuation." *Collected Works*, vol. 11, 23. Princeton, NJ: Princeton University Press, 2000.

Kauffman, Stuart A. *Reinventing the Sacred: A New View of Science, Reason, and Religion.* New York: Basic Books, 2008.

Keller, Catherine. *Cloud of the Impossible: Negative Theology and Planetary Entanglement.* New York: Columbia University Press, 2015.

Kelly, Kevin. *The Inevitable: Understanding the Twelve Technological Forces That Will Shape Our Future.* New York: Penguin Publishing Group, 2016.

Laszlo, Ervin. *Quantum Shift in a Global Brain: How the New Scientific Reality Can Change Us and Our World.* Rochester, VT: Inner Traditions, 2008.

Le Grice, Keiron. *Archetypal Reflection: Insights and Ideas from Jungian Psychology.* New York: Muswell Hill Press, 2016.

Lightman, Alan. *A Sense of the Mysterious: Science and the Human Spirit.* New York: Pantheon Books, 2005.

McFadden, Johnjoe, and Jim Al-Khalili. *Life on the Edge: The Coming of Age of Quantum Biology.* New York: Crown Publishers, 2014.

McGrath, Alister E. *A Fine-Tuned Universe: The Quest for God in Science and Theology.* Louisville, KY: Westminster John Knox, 2009.

McIntosh, Steve. *The Presence of the Infinite: The Spiritual Experience of Beauty, Truth, and Goodness.* Wheaton, IL: Quest Books, 2015.

Miller, Jeffrey C. *The Transcendent Function: Jung's Model of Psychological Growth through Dialogue With the Unconscious.* Albany: State University of New York (SUNY) Press, 2004.

Naess, Arne. *The Ecology of Wisdom: Writings by Arne Naess.* Edited by Alan Drengson and Bill Devall. Berkeley, CA: Counterpoint, 2010.

Newell, John Philip. *The Rebirthing of God: Christianity's Struggle for New Beginnings.* Woodstock, VT: Skylight Paths Publishing, 2015.

Olson, Edwin E. *Finding Reality: Four Ways of Knowing*. Bloomington, IN: Archway Publishing, 2014.

Olson, Edwin E., and Glenda H. Eoyang. *Facilitating Organization Change: Lessons from Complexity Science*. San Francisco: Jossey-Bass/Pfeiffer, 2001.

Orr, Emma Restall. *The Wakeful World: Animism, Mind, and the Self in Nature*. Winchester, UK: Moon Books, 2012.

Phillips, Jan. *No Ordinary Time: The Rise of Spiritual Intelligence and Evolutionary Creativity*. San Diego: Living Kindness Foundation, 2011.

Reho, James. *Tantric Jesus: The Erotic Heart of Early Christianity*. Rochester, VT: Destiny Books, 2017.

Rohr, Richard. *Immortal Diamond: The Search for Our True Self*. San Francisco: Jossey-Bass, 2013.

Rothluebber, Francis. *Who Creates the Future: Discovering the Essential Energy of Co-Creation*. Idyllwild, CA: Womenspace, 2016.

Rovelli, Carlo. *Seven Brief Lessons on Physics*. New York: Penguin Riverhead Books, 2014.

Russell, Heidi Ann. *Quantum Shift: Theological and Pastoral Implications of Contemporary Developments in Science*. Collegeville, MN: Liturgical Press, 2015.

Sanguin, Bruce. *The Way of the Wind: The Path and Practice of Evolutionary Christian Mysticism*. Vancouver: Viriditas Press, 2015.

Seed, John. "The Ecological Self." *EarthLight Magazine #53*, vol. 14, no. 4 (Spring 2005).

Senge, Peter M., C. Otto Scharmer, Joseph Jaworski, and Betty Sue Flowers. *Presence: Human Purpose and the Field of the Future*. Cambridge, MA: The Society for Organizational Learning, 2004.

Sharma, Kriti. *Interdependence: Biology and Beyond*. New York: Fordham University Press, 2015.

Stein, Murray. *Practicing Wholeness: Analytical Psychology and Jungian Thought*. New York: Continuum, 1996.

Teasdale, Wayne. *The Mystic Heart: Discovering a Universal Spirituality in the World's Religion*. Novato, CA: New World Library, 1999, 2001.

Teilhard de Chardin, Pierre. *The Divine Milieu*. New York: Harper Perennial Modern Classics, 2001.

————. *Toward the Future*. San Diego: Mariner Books 2002.

Tolle, Eckhart. *A New Earth: Awakening to Your Life's Purpose*. New York: Penguin Books, 2005.

Tydell, Mallary, and Royce Holladay. *Simple Rules: A Radical Inquiry into Self*. Apache Junction, AZ: Gold Canyon Press, 2011.

Underhill, Evelyn. *Practical Mysticism*. New York: Dutton, 1914.

Ward, Keith, *The Big Questions in Science and Religion*. West Conshohocken, PA: Templeton Press, 2009.

Wilber, Ken. *The Religion of Tomorrow*. Boulder, CO: Shambhala, 2017.

Wilczek, Frank. *A Beautiful Question: Finding Nature's Deep Design*. New York: Penguin, 2015.

Yong, Ed. *I Contain Multitudes: The Microbes within Us and a Grander View of Life*. New York: HarperCollins, 2016.

Young-Eisendrath, Polly, and Melvin E. Miller, eds. *The Psychology of Mature Spirituality: Integrity, Wisdom, Transcendence*. Philadelphia: Taylor and Francis, 2000.

Zukov, Gary. *The Seat of the Soul*. New York: Simon and Schuster, 1989.

Index